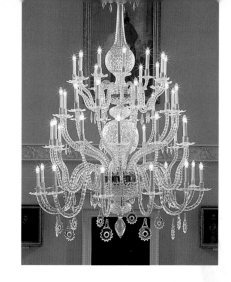

THE MUSEUM OF COSTUME & ASSEMBLY ROOMS BATH

THE AUTHORISED GUIDE

For centuries Bath has been a centre of fashion, attracting visitors to its spa and social diversions.

The Assembly Rooms are one of Bath's finest Georgian buildings and still central to the city's social life today. Very appropriately, they also house the Museum of Costume and its internationally renowned collection of fashionable dress.

Fabric – of architecture, social life and dress – is the theme of this Guide. It unites two aspects of our heritage: the Assembly Rooms, a National Trust building leased to Bath & North East Somerset Council, and the Museum of Costume which is owned and managed by the Council.

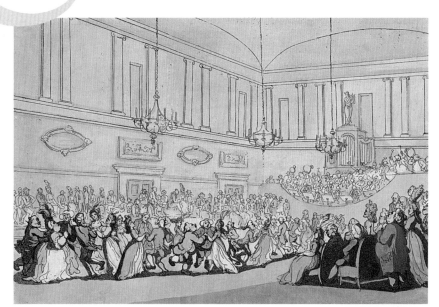

Country dancing in the Ballroom, 1798
Watercolour by Thomas Rowlandson from THE COMFORTS OF BATH.

Above:
The chandelier, designed by Jonathan Collett, in the Octagon

Right:
Eighteenth century gallery
Museum of Costume display.

Opposite:
The Entrance Hall

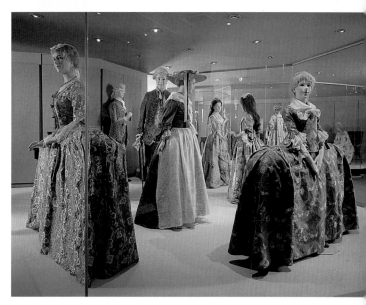

W9-CIL-605

'Polite Society': Bath in the Eighteenth Century

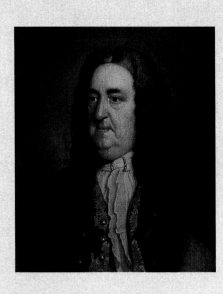

Richard 'Beau' Nash (1674-1761)
Painted in 1745 at the end of his reign over fashionable Bath by Adriaen Charpentiers. Somewhat surprisingly, he favoured unfashionable dress, fastening his stock with a diamond buckle and wearing a white three-cornered hat.

'Beau' Nash and Bath
Visitors had been coming to Bath since Roman times to take the mineral waters for their health, when the 28-year-old Richard Nash arrived in about 1703. By 1706 'Beau' Nash had become the city's Master of Ceremonies and within a decade had transformed Bath into the resort of choice not just for the rich, but for the whole of 'polite society'. He did this by laying down a code of behaviour – his famous 'Rules'. These encouraged sociability between the growing gentry class and the aristocratic elite, who had traditionally kept themselves apart from the rest of society.

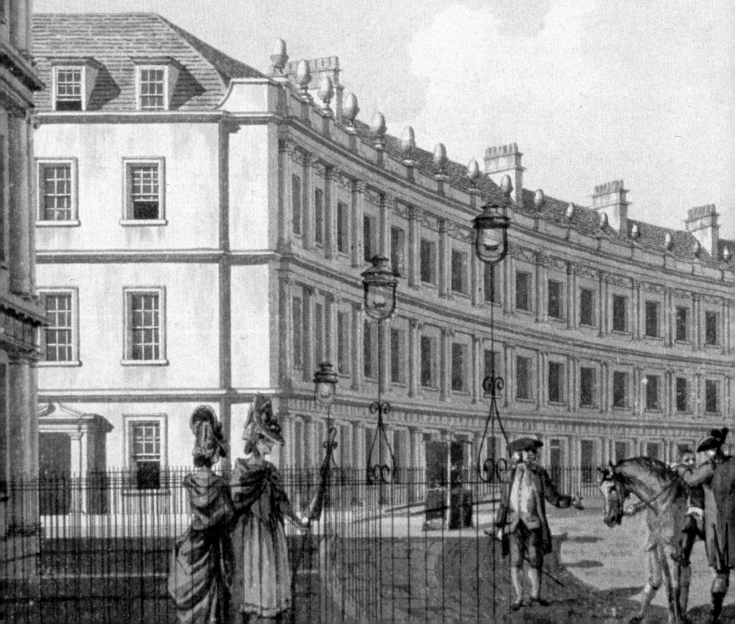

> *'Bath is to me a new world*
> *– All is gaiety, good-humour,*
> *and diversion.'*
>
> Lydia Melford in HUMPHRY CLINKER, 1771

Nash forbade hard drinking and the wearing of swords, which often led to duels. He also set out a common dress code and rules of etiquette that made the less fashionably minded feel at home. Nash was so successful that the population rose from 3,000 in 1700 to 35,000 a century later, greatly swelled by visitors during the Bath season, which ran from October to early June.

Building the New City
To cater for these people and their new way of life, the property developer Ralph Allen and the architect John Wood the Elder built the city we see today. The new terraces and crescents provided plenty of apartments for visitors to rent, the streets a fashionable setting in which they could promenade in comfort and safety. Nash frowned on private entertainment, encouraging visitors to mingle in public, at the Theatre, Pump Room and the Assembly Rooms.

The Circus
Watercolour by Thomas Malton, 1784. Improved street lighting and paving made Bath one of the safest English cities in which to walk at night in the eighteenth century – essential to the success of the Assembly Rooms.

RULES
by general Consent determined

I. That a visit of ceremony at coming to Bath, and another at going away, is all that is expected or desired by ladies of quality and fashion – except impertinents.

II. That ladies coming to the ball appoint a time for their footmen's coming to wait on them home, to prevent disturbances and inconveniences to themselves and others.

III. That gentlemen of fashion never appearing in a morning before the ladies in gowns and caps, shew breeding and respect.

IV. That no person take it ill that any one goes to another's play or breakfast, and not to their's – except captious by nature.

V. That no gentleman give his tickets for the balls to any but gentlewomen – N.B. Unless he has none of his acquaintance.

VI. That gentlemen crowding before ladies at the ball, shew ill-manners; and that none do so for the future – except such as respect nobody but themselves.

VII. That no gentleman or lady take it ill that another dances before them – except such as have no pretence to dance at all.

VIII. That the elder ladies and children be contented with a second bench at the ball, as being past or not come to perfection.

IX. That the younger ladies take notice how many eyes observe them – N.B. This does not extend to the Have-at-Alls.

X. That all whisperers of lies and scandal be taken for their authors.

XI. That all repeaters of such lies and scandal be shunned by all company – except such as have been guilty of the same crime.
N.B. Several men of no character, old women and young ones of questioned reputation, are great authors of lies in this place, being of the sect of Levellers.

'BEAU' NASH, 1742

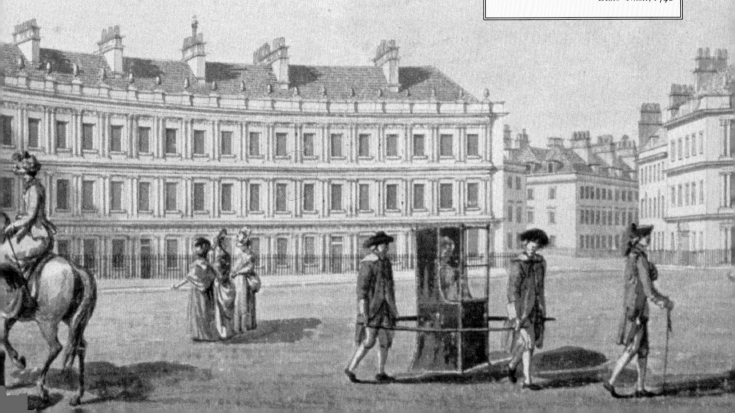

Building the new Assembly Rooms

Rival Schemes

In the 1760s there were already two Assembly Rooms in Bath: Harrison's (later Simpson's), which had been built in 1708 at the instigation of 'Beau' Nash; and Lindsey's (later Wiltshire's), designed in 1728 by John Wood the Elder. But, as Wood himself commented in 1742, *'Neither ... can be called, or even made a compleat Building.'* They were old-fashioned, too small for the rapidly growing city, and inconveniently far from the new and more fashionable upper town. So he proposed a purpose-built suite of rooms to rival those built in 1731–2 in York by Lord Burlington, but nothing came of this scheme.

In 1765 his son, John Wood the Younger, suggested combining new rooms with a tavern and a coffee-house on a site beyond the north-west corner of Queen Square. However, a tavern was thought 'an improper appendage to a set of Public Rooms' and this plan also lapsed. Robert Adam designed a huge and very ambitious rival scheme, probably with the encouragement of William Pulteney, but once again it was turned down, this time as too expensive. Finally, Wood succeeded in getting a revised plan accepted.

Robert Adam's scheme for the Assembly Rooms
This grandiose design was rejected as too expensive.

Raising the Money

Wood raised the finance through a 'tontine' subscription, whereby the shares of those who die are added to the holdings of the survivors and the last survivor inherits all. The lists opened in November 1768, and by April 1769 £14,000 had been raised from 53 individuals; the total cost of £20,000 made the new Assembly Rooms the biggest investment in a single building in eighteenth-century Bath. The foundation stone was laid on 26 May 1769, and fitting out the interior finished in 1771.

Plan of the Assembly Rooms

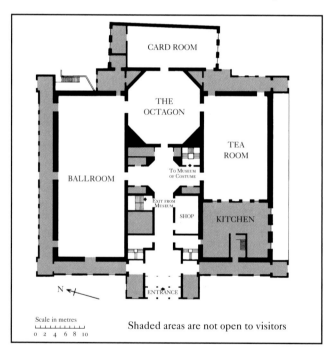

CARD ROOM

THE OCTAGON

TEA ROOM

BALLROOM

To Museum of Costume

Exit from Museum

SHOP

KITCHEN

N

ENTRANCE

Scale in metres
0 2 4 6 8 10

Shaded areas are not open to visitors

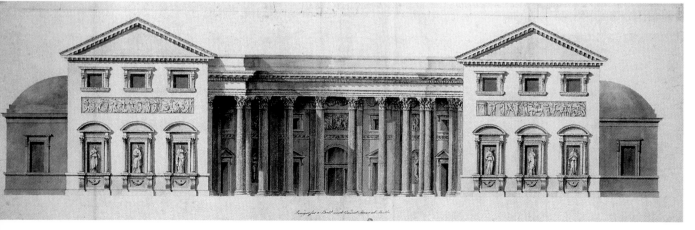

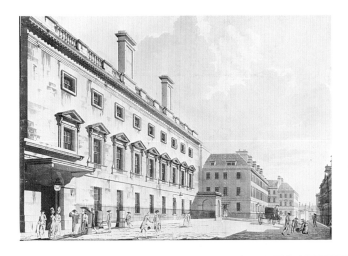

The Alfred Street front
Aquatint after Thomas Malton, c.1779.

Design and Decoration

Wood chose a secluded site between Bennett and Alfred Streets to the north-east of his father's Circus. His plan was essentially U-shaped, with the main entrance (for those who arrived on foot or by sedan chair) on the west front under a single-storey Doric portico projecting from between the tall balancing blocks of the Ballroom and Tea Room. Sedan chairs could be left in the colonnade that ran along the north side of the Ballroom. Those who came by carriage alighted at the north-west and south-west doors.

In comparison with the grand interior, the exterior is distinctly plain, the only relief being provided by the pedimented windows on the first storey and the broad entablature and balustrade running round the main blocks.

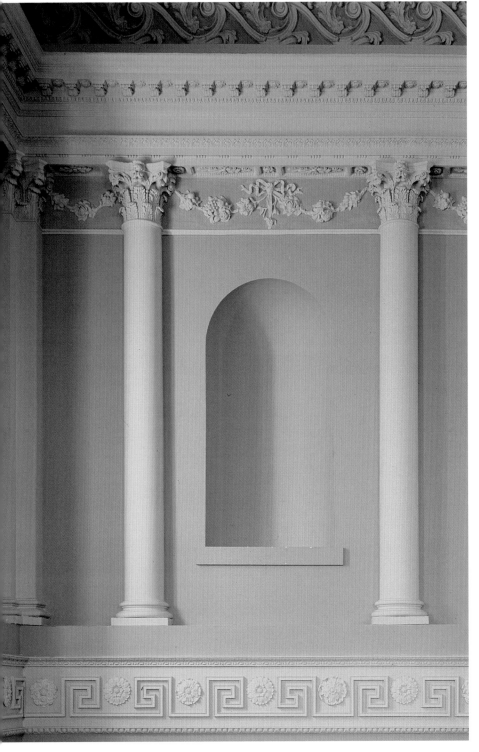

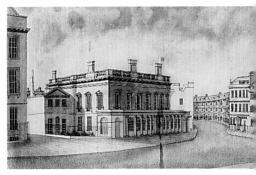

The Ballroom
The Corinthian columns, ornate swags and Vitruvian scroll are in marked contrast to the plain exterior of the Assembly Rooms.

The Bennett Street front
The Ballroom is behind the glazed corridor for sedan chairs. This pen and ink drawing by William Blackamore rather fancifully also includes the Circus.

Life in the Assembly Rooms

Opening Night

The New, or Upper, Assembly Rooms opened on 30 September 1771 with a Ridotto (a combined dance and concert). Captain William Wade presided as Master of Ceremonies. Complimentary tickets were sent to the Mayor, the two Justices of the Peace and three to Thomas Gainsborough, doubtless in appreciation of the gift of Captain Wade's portrait. For everyone else it was *'One Guinea to admit One Gentleman and two Ladies at seven shillings each'*. The Management Committee ordered *'the doors to open at seven o'clock, the side boards at nine o'clock and to shut at Twelve'*.
The caterers, Messrs Kuliff and Fitzwater, were instructed *'to furnish all the ornaments for the front Table, the Tables of the side board and the beau-fretts'*, and to supply *'cakes, jellies etc.'* Life in the Rooms was under way.

Assemblies

An 'assembly' was defined in 1751 as *'a stated and general meeting of the polite persons of both sexes, for the sake of conversation, gallantry, news and play'*. Guests amused themselves at cards, drank tea or just walked around talking and flirting.
These pursuits were not new in themselves, but hitherto they had taken place in a sequence which everyone had to follow. The guests did one thing at a time and they all did it together. At an assembly, dancing, tea-drinking and cards went on at the same time spread through different rooms, if possible. Hence the enthusiasm for the younger Wood's Assembly Rooms. As their names suggest, each principal room had a specific purpose – dancing, cards and refreshments – but they could all adapt for other functions.

Dress Ball.

1811---1812.

SUBSCRIPTION for 24 BALLS,
EVERY MONDAY DURING THE SEASON,
ON THE FOLLOWING TERMS:

A Subscription of FOURTEEN SHILLINGS will entitle the Subscriber to Admission each Ball Night.

A Subscription of TWENTY-SIX SHILLINGS will entitle the Subscriber to Admission each Ball Night, and also to TWO TICKETS, *transferable to Ladies only*.

Such transferable Tickets to be respectively endorsed with the Names of the Subscriber, and the Lady to whom transferred.

Every Person to pay SIXPENCE on Admission to each Ball for Tea.

Non-Subscriber's Admittance *Five Shillings.*

☞ *The SUBSCRIBERS are respectfully requested to observe, that their Subscriptions cease when they leave Bath; and it would be of much Public Utility, if they would be pleased to give Notice at the Rooms of their Departure, which would prevent their Tickets being improperly used.*

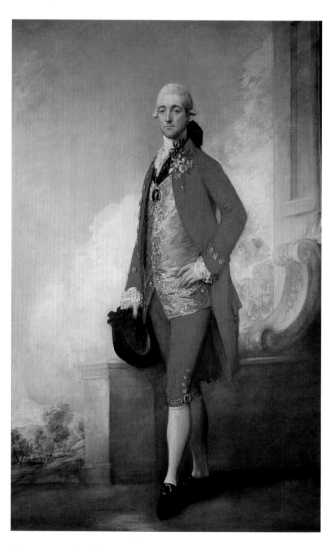

The rooms lead into each other in sequence, but each is linked independently to the central vestibule.

Subscription Rates

In Bath the festivities alternated between the New and the Lower Assembly Rooms. At the New Rooms there was a Dress Ball on Mondays, for which the subscription for the season in the eighteenth century was one guinea (three tickets); a concert on Wednesdays with the gentlemen's subscriptions also at one guinea (again, three tickets) and the ladies', half a guinea; and a Cotillion Ball (country dancing) on Thursdays, gentlemen's subscription at half a guinea (one ticket) and partners at five shillings each. In addition the Rooms were open every day *'for the company to walk and play at cards'* for a subscription of ten shillings for gentlemen and five shillings for ladies.

Captain William Wade

Wade was Master of Ceremonies in Bath from 1769 to 1777. Like Nash, he published rules of behaviour and dress for guests, *'it being absolutely necessary that a propriety of dress should be observed at so polite an assembly as that at Bath.'* He was painted here in 1771 by Gainsborough, the most fashionable artist in the city and then living nearby in the Circus.

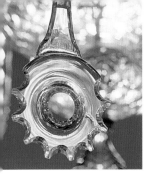

Lighting the Rooms

A cut-glass drop from Jonathan Collett's Octagon chandelier

William Parker's trade card
Parker later went on to supply chandeliers to the Prince Regent for his London mansion, Carlton House.

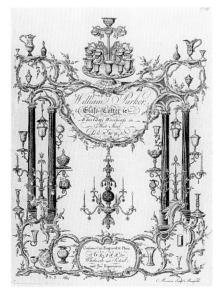

One of William Parker's Ballroom chandeliers

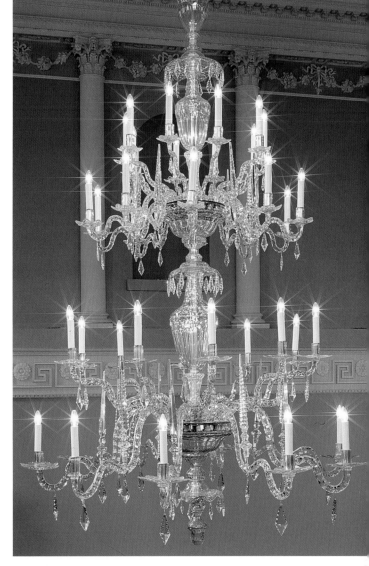

Dancing by Candlelight

As balls did not start until 6 and the season spanned the winter months, good artificial lighting was vital. The Furnishing Committee commissioned Mr William Evill to make '*30 pair of the best plated Candlesticks according to the pattern now produced at the Price of £3.10.0 a pair*'. But their single largest purchase – at £999 – was of the nine great chandeliers, which are among the most important to have survived from the eighteenth century. On 15 August 1771 Jonathan Collett quoted £400 for supplying five cut-glass chandeliers for the Ballroom. They were up in time for the opening of the Rooms in September, but the following month disaster struck when '*one of the arms of the chandeliers in the Ballroom fell down during the time the company was dancing*', narrowly missing Gainsborough. What could be salvaged from the set was made up into a single chandelier, which now hangs in the Octagon.

The Committee turned to William Parker of Fleet Street in London, who had already been called in to make the Tea Room

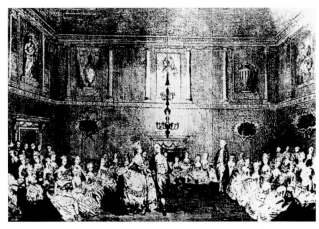

chandeliers, to provide replacements for the Ballroom. Parker's designs were altogether more modern than Collett's and made his reputation. Keeping the chandeliers lit was a time-consuming and extremely expensive business: the bill for candles and oil was £556.3.8 for the first season alone.

The Rooms at Night
This eighteenth-century engraving of the Ballroom gives a unique impression of how it must have looked by candlelight.

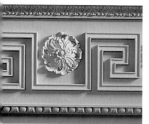

The Ballroom: Dancing

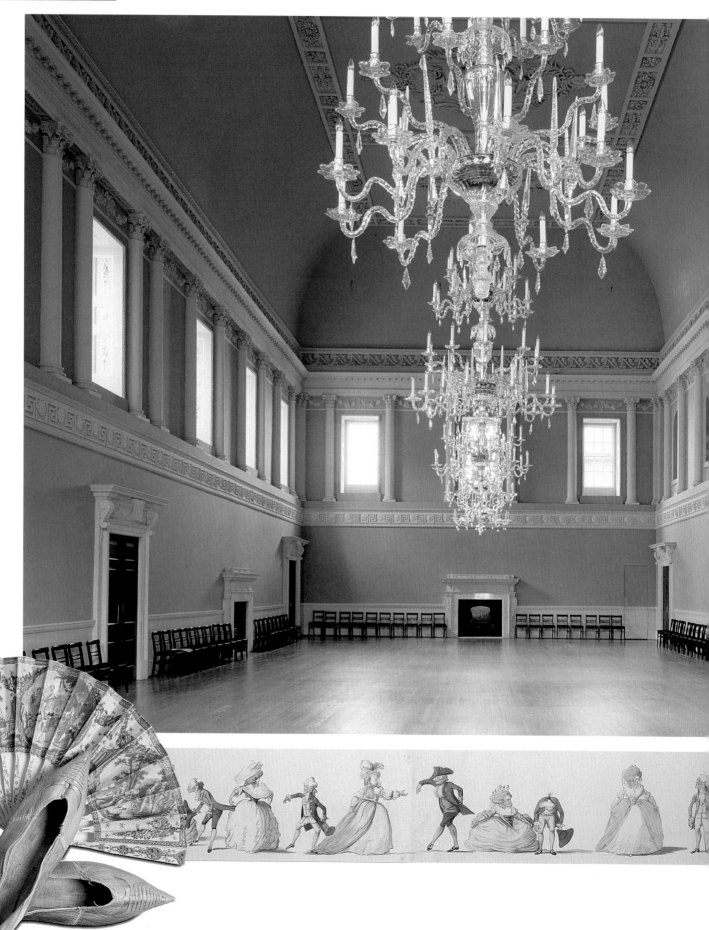

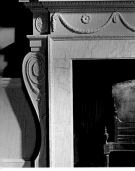

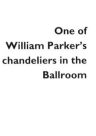

Neo-classical chimneypiece with swags and rosettes

One of William Parker's chandeliers in the Ballroom

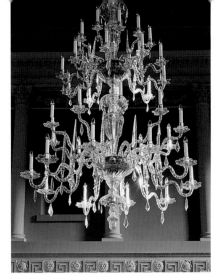

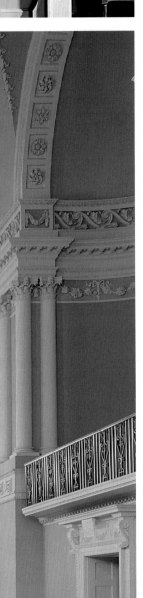

'The Ballroom is 105ft 8in long, 42ft 8in wide, and 42ft 6in high, wainscotted to a height of 4ft, over which the stucco rises 8ft 6in to a rich fretwork on which stands the sub-plinth of the order, which is Corinthian and consists of forty columns and pilasters 12ft high, with its entablature curiously enriched; above which is a plinth ornamented with a rich Vitruvian scroll, from whence rises the cove 11ft 6in high, the angle bracket of which forms a quarter-circle. From the front line of the cove into the ceiling is a soffit, divided into compartments which are decorated with garlands, palm and laurel branches, festoons etc.'

THE NEW BATH GUIDE, 1772

An Ideal Space

The Ballroom is the largest eighteenth-century room in Bath. Today it seems somewhat empty but we must imagine it in the eighteenth century packed with as many as 800 dancers. The fireplaces provided a quick burst of warmth for early arrivals. As the dancing got under way, the heat rose rapidly and was absorbed by the high ceiling, and through the upper storey windows. The lower walls were left deliberately bare, as they were usually obscured by tiers of movable benches. In 1772 Mr Brimble contracted *'that himself and Men will put up and take away the Platforms and Orchestra for the Balls, & Concerts, and place the settees.'* William Parker's chandeliers provided the principal decoration.

Dress Balls and Country Dances

Dress Balls were held once a week and began at 6, when the eleven musicians in the first-floor gallery struck up. Between 6 and 8 there were minuets, a stately dance performed by couples alone: *'It is often remarked by Foreigners that the English Nation of both sexes look as grave when they are dancing, as if they were attending the Solemnity of a Funeral.'* The more energetic country dances followed between 8 and 9 and required rather freer dress, as the Rooms' rules noted: *'No Lady dance country-dances in a hoop of any kind and those who choose to pull their hoops off, will be assisted by proper servants in an apartment for that purpose.'*

At 9 the dancers moved to the Tea Room for refreshment. The entertainment continued with further country dances till 11, when the evening ended.

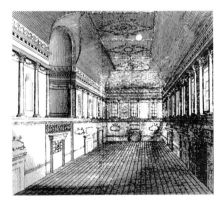

Engraving of the Ballroom, c.1784

The Long Minuet at Bath
Engraving after Henry William Bunbury, 1787.

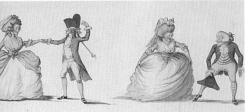

But hark! now they strike the melodious string,
The vaulted roof echoes, the mansions all ring;
At the sound of the hautboy, the bass and the fiddle,
Sir Boreas Blubber steps forth in the middle,
Like a holy-hock, noble, majestic, and tall,
Sir Boreas Blubber first opens the ball ...
How he puts on his hat, with a smile on his face,
And delivers his hand with an exquisite grace!
How genteely he offers Miss Carrot before us,
Miss Carrot Fitz-Oozer, a niece of Lord Porus!
How nimbly he paces, how active and light!
One never can judge of a man at first sight!
But as near as I guess, from the size of his calf,
He may weigh about twenty-three stone and a half.

Christopher Anstey, THE NEW BATH GUIDE, 1766

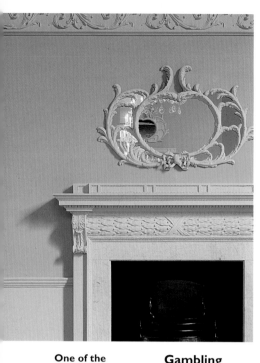

One of the Octagon mirrors
In April 1771 Mr Dear supplied *'sixteen small Girandoles according to the Pattern now produced at £3.16.0 each'.*

Gambling

Gambling was endemic in early eighteenth-century Britain. As the historian William Lecky wrote, *'At Bath ... it reigned supreme; and the physicians even recommended it to their patients as a form of distraction.... Among fashionable ladies the passion was quite as strong as among men, and the professor of whist and quadrille became a regular attendant at their levées.'* Nash had mixed feelings on the subject. Although he earned his living as a professional gambler, he was concerned about the obvious dangers of playing for high stakes and tried to help heavy losers. He himself was eventually ruined by the laws passed in 1739 and 1745 to ban Faro, Basset, Hazard, Ace of Hearts and Even-Odd.

The Octagon

This was a card room before the room of that name was added. Here parties gathered at tables supplied by Mr Coxhead, covered with cloths from Mr Danvers to deal whist cards *'masked with the Moghul's head'*. On Sundays, when card-playing was not permitted, the company could sit back and listen to the organ which once stood in the musicians' gallery above the main entrance.

The Card Room

The Card Room was added in 1777, demonstrating the popularity of the Assembly Rooms as a convivial meeting place. The architect of this simply decorated room is not known. The walls are divided into tall panels up to the delicate cornice, with windows set in oval, palm-fringed frames. It was the only room to escape damage in 1942, and now serves as a refreshment room and bar.

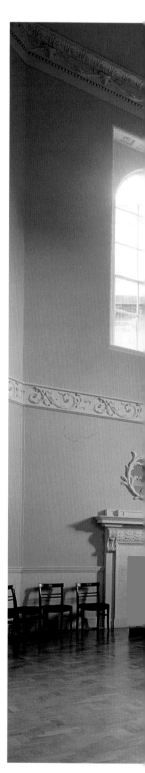

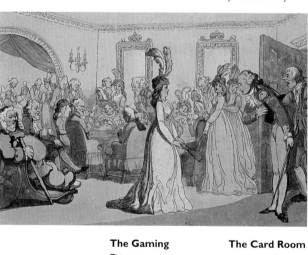

The Gaming Room
From Thomas Rowlandson's THE PLEASURES OF BATH.

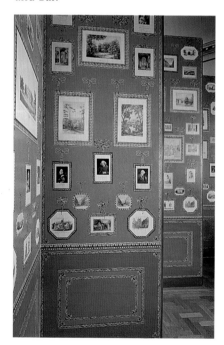

The Card Room Screen
Designed by Nicola Wingate-Saul in imitation of eighteenth-century print rooms.

'An octagon of 48ft diameter, [it] has four marble chimney-pieces properly ornamented, is wainscotted, stuccoed and ceiled nearly in the same manner as the Ballroom, and in the stucco are ornamental frames for portrait paintings [now gone]. This room has two doors besides that which fronts the entrance, one of which opens to the [Ballroom], and the other to the Tea Room. In this room is a fine portrait of Captain Wade, late Master of Ceremonies, painted by Mr Gainsborough.'

THE NEW BATH GUIDE, 1772

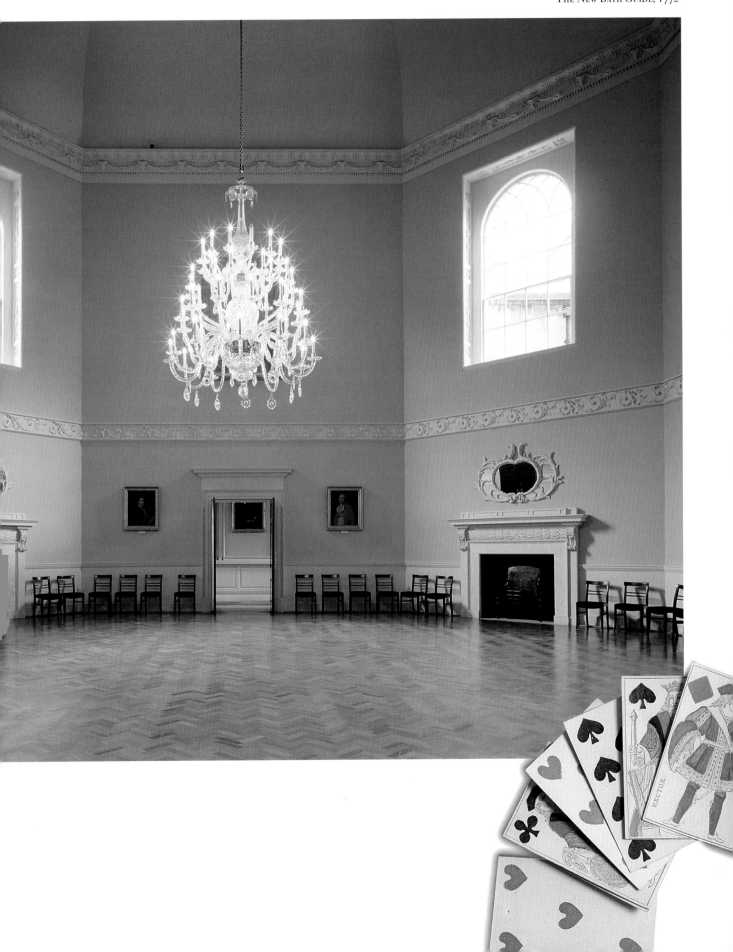

The Tea Room: Taking Tea and Making Music

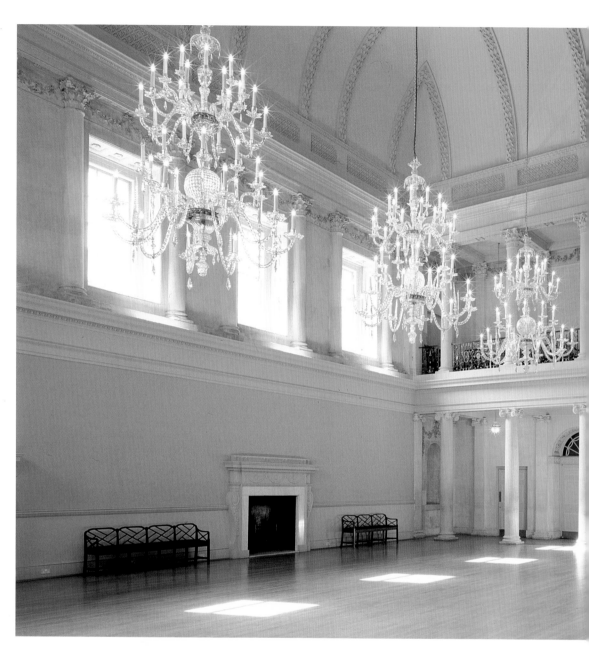

'The Tea Room is 60ft long, and 42ft wide. At the west end is a colonnade of the Ionic order, 7ft wide, consisting of six columns and ten pilasters 11ft 6in high, with its enriched entablature which continues round the room. These support the Corinthian order of equal number, and the orchestra, the front of which is bounded with a rich gilded iron railing that extends from column to column. From hence the Corinthian order continues round the room and consists of thirty columns and pilasters, with their capitals, festoons, etc., curiously carved in Bath stone. The entablature is of stucco, above which is a pedestal wrought in mosaic-work, from which rises a cove, the line of which is relieved by a swelling soffit of laurel leaves interspersed with berries, which are continued, to and from, across and along the ceiling, rolling under each other and forming by their intersection the most beautiful network, embellished with garlands, laurels, palm branches, festoons and wreaths of flowers.'

THE NEW BATH
GUIDE, 1772

**The Tea Room in
1805**
Aquatint after
John Nattes.

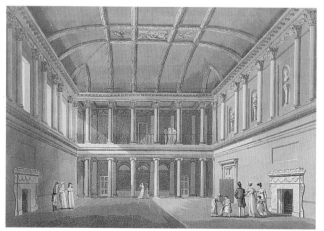

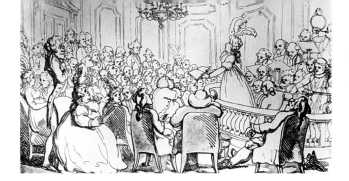

The Concert
From Rowlandson's THE PLEASURES OF BATH.

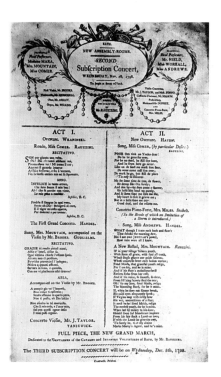

Programme for a concert organised by Rauzzini in 1798

Food and Drink

In the eighteenth century the Tea Room was used primarily for refreshments and concerts. Meals were served throughout the day, from 'public breakfasts' ordered by fashionable visitors for their friends and acquaintances, to supper during Dress Balls. Food was laid out on side-tables behind the screen and for the blue-stocking Mrs Montagu included *'sweetmeats, jellies, wine, biscuits, cold ham and turkey'*. Tea was the favourite drink, usually drunk as a weak infusion without milk, but sometimes with arrack (fermented cocoa) and lemon. A foreign visitor noted that, in contrast to the rest of the country, at Bath *'the Tea-Parties are extremely gay'*. Jerry Melford's account of a tea party in HUMPHRY CLINKER suggests that things could sometimes get out of hand:

'The tea-drinking passed as usual, and the company having risen from the tables, were sauntering in groupes, in expectation of the signal for attack, when the bell beginning to ring, they flew with eagerness to the dessert, and the whole place was instantly in commotion. There was nothing but justling, scrambling, pulling, snatching, struggling, scolding, and screaming.'

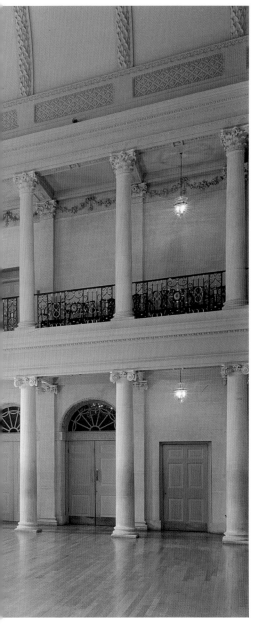

Music

Subscription concerts were a regular part of life in the Rooms. These were directed at first by Thomas Linley, the leading musician in Bath. He was succeeded around 1777 by the Italian male soprano and composer Venanzio Rauzzini in collaboration with the violinist Franz Lamotte. Mozart had written for Rauzzini, who brought many of the finest singers of the day to Bath. The most distinguished visitor was Joseph Haydn, who wrote a canon in praise of Rauzzini's dog, Turk.

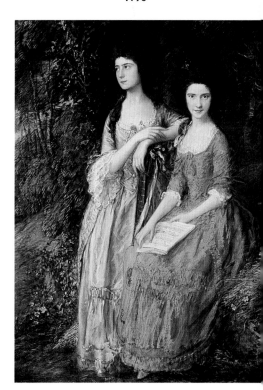

Elizabeth Ann (left) and Mary Linley
Thomas Linley's daughters both became successful singers. Taught by their father, they performed from an early age in his subscription concerts in the Assembly Rooms. In 1772 Elizabeth caused a scandal by eloping with the playwright Richard Brinsley Sheridan. She was considered the finest English soprano of her day. Portrait by Thomas Gainsborough.

The Nineteenth Century

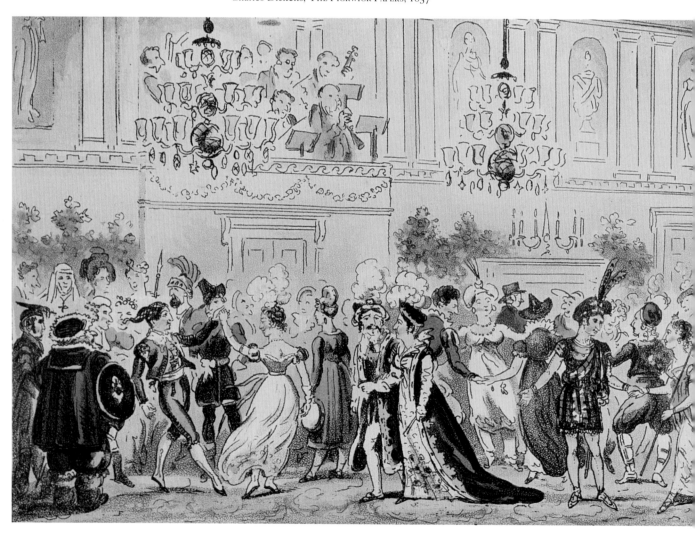

The Assembly Rooms from the north-west
A mid-nineteenth-century lithograph.

'In the ball-room, the long card-room, the octagonal card-room, the staircases, and the passages, the hum of many voices, and the sound of many feet, were perfectly bewildering. Dresses rustled, feathers waved, lights shone, and jewels sparkled. There was the music – not of the quadrille band, for it had not yet commenced; but the music of soft tiny footsteps, with now and then a clear merry laugh – low and gentle, but very pleasant to hear in a female voice, whether in Bath or elsewhere. Brilliant eyes, lighted up with pleasurable expectation, gleamed from every side; and look where you would, some exquisite form glided gracefully through the throng, and was no sooner lost than it was replaced by another, as dainty, and bewitching.'

Charles Dickens, THE PICKWICK PAPERS, 1837

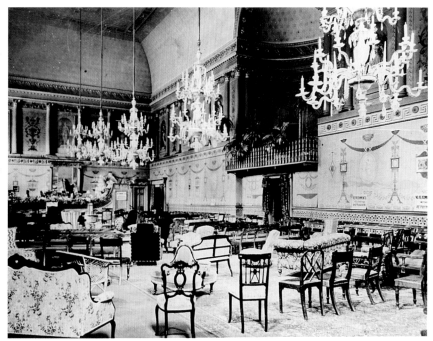

The Ballroom c.1890
In the nineteenth century a series of new decorative schemes were devised to enliven the bare lower walls of the main rooms. This photograph shows Edward Bell's scheme of 1879. The ceiling and cove were blue, the upper walls pearl grey with arabesques between the niches, the lower walls 'warm salmon' with more arabesques, and the dado heavily stencilled in 'rich chocolate and dark cinnamon colours'.

The Fancy Ball
Engraving by Robert Cruikshank, 1825.

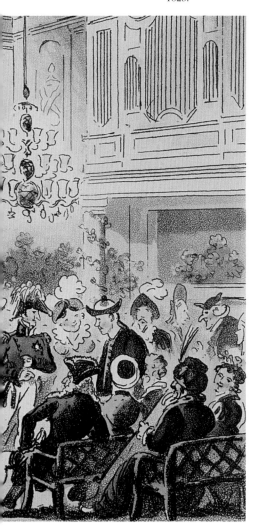

Decline

During the nineteenth century Bath lost its pre-eminence amongst the fashionable resorts. It was the era of the seaside towns like Brighton, and, for the dedicated invalid, the exotic European spas. This decline is reflected in the fortunes of the Assembly Rooms. However, concerts remained popular. Local musicians maintained a high standard vitalised by touring celebrities such as Johann Strauss the Elder and Franz Liszt. Popular entertainments included a visit from General Tom Thumb and several public readings by Dickens. In the 1860s the Rooms were also used for conferences of learned societies. The importance of the Master of Ceremonies dwindled, indeed the job was vacant from 1864 to 1874.

Francis Kilvert visits Bath

The parties continued, but the tone was rather different, judging from Francis Kilvert's description of a reception there in 1873: '*Some 3000 people were present and yet there was plenty of space to walk about in these noble rooms. We arrived at 9 and left at midnight. There was a band, tea, coffee, ices, champagne cup, claret cup, sandwiches, and speeches by the Bishop of Peterborough, the Bishop of Manchester, the Rector of Bath, and Mr Randall, Vicar of All Saints, Clifton ...*'

The Rooms become a Cinema

By the end of the nineteenth century the Rooms were competing with the newly enlarged Pump Room and hotels with large public rooms. Soon the proprietors met financial difficulties. By selling the Gainsborough in 1903 (bought back in 1988), they staved off bankruptcy for a while. Major Simpson, the last Master of Ceremonies, struggled to bring life to the Rooms with a series of balls in eighteenth-century dress. When the Great War came, the building was occupied the Royal Flying Corps. Subsequently the Ballroom became a cinema, and most of the furniture was sold in 1920.

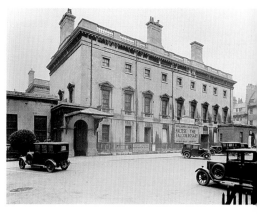

Picture Palace
The Rooms in use as a cinema.

Ruin and Restoration

The Rooms Rescued

The sad decline of the Rooms ended in 1931, when they were purchased by the Society for the Protection of Ancient Buildings through the generosity of Ernest Cook and given to the National Trust. The Trust let the Rooms to the Bath City Council at a nominal rent, on condition the building was restored to its original state. The work was carried out by the local firm of J. Long & Sons, and supervised by Mowbray Green, the architect and architectural historian. Recent accretions were demolished, tarnished decorations swept away, and the Rooms emerged trim, uncluttered and shining in cream and white paint with lavish gilding. On 19 October 1938 they were reopened with a grand eighteenth-century costume ball. Four years later, on 25 April 1942, Bath was heavily bombed, and the Rooms were reduced to a roofless shell.

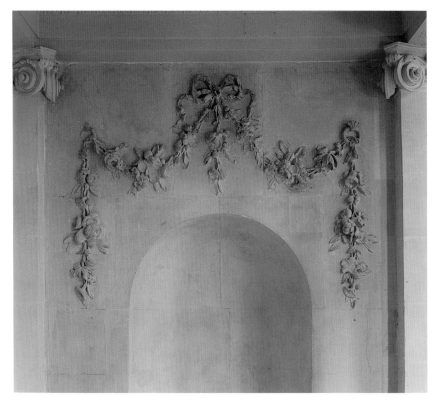

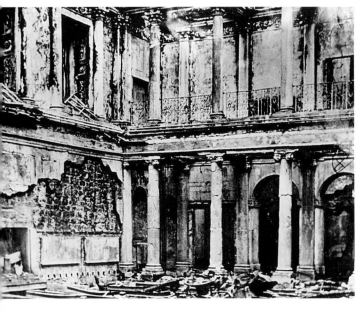

Bombed out
The Tea Room
after the 1942 blitz.

Post-War Revival

The Trust decided on a faithful restoration of the Assembly Rooms and in 1946 brought in Sir Albert Richardson, a connoisseur of Georgian architecture, to supervise the project. Complex negotiations held up work until 1956, when the roofs were rebuilt by traditional methods, incorporating massive beams of Douglas Fir some 62ft long. While being obliged to install modern services, Sir Albert was determined to reconstruct the three great rooms with their original features and proportions. However, lack of money meant that the ornate ceiling decoration had to be re-instated in fibrous plaster rather than traditional lime plaster, following surviving fragments and old photographs. With a meagre budget of little over £4,000, the set-designer Oliver Messel evolved colour schemes which brought a festive air to the Rooms.

Fire Damage

The stonework in the Tea Room was tinged pink by the fire that followed the 1942 blitz. In the absence of documentary evidence, this forms the basis for the present colour scheme of pinks and browns.

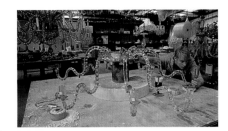

Sparking anew
The chandeliers undergoing restoration in the workshops of R. Wilkinson & Sons.

The Ballroom ceiling
The ornate plasterwork was taken down and carefully cleaned.

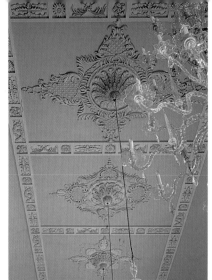

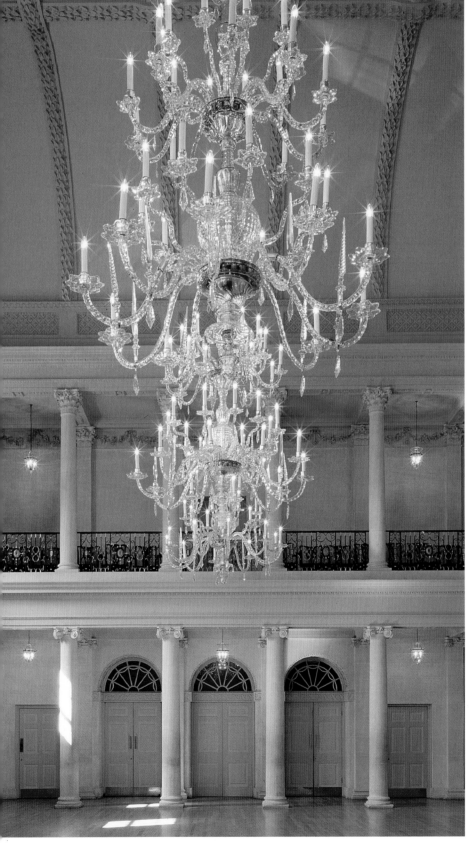

Recent Restorations

In the 1970s, thanks to a gift of £40,000 from Mr and Mrs Kenneth Levy, the Trust and the City Council were able to make radical improvements to the Rooms and to the Museum of Costume which has been displayed here since 1963. David Mlinaric redecorated the principal rooms, deciding on a simple treatment based on original colour samples discovered in the City Archives.

On 13 October 1987 a large section of plaster crashed to the ground from the Ballroom ceiling. Investigation revealed serious faults in other parts of the plasterwork, and it was decided to commission the David Brain Partnership and Wickens Construction to embark on a thorough restoration programme costing the City Council over £3 million. Richardson's decorative plasterwork was taken down and repaired, the Rooms were repainted largely following David Mlinaric's scheme, and the chandeliers cleaned and repaired. In January 1991 the Rooms reopened, ready to entertain visitors once again, as they have for the past 200 years.

The Tea Room

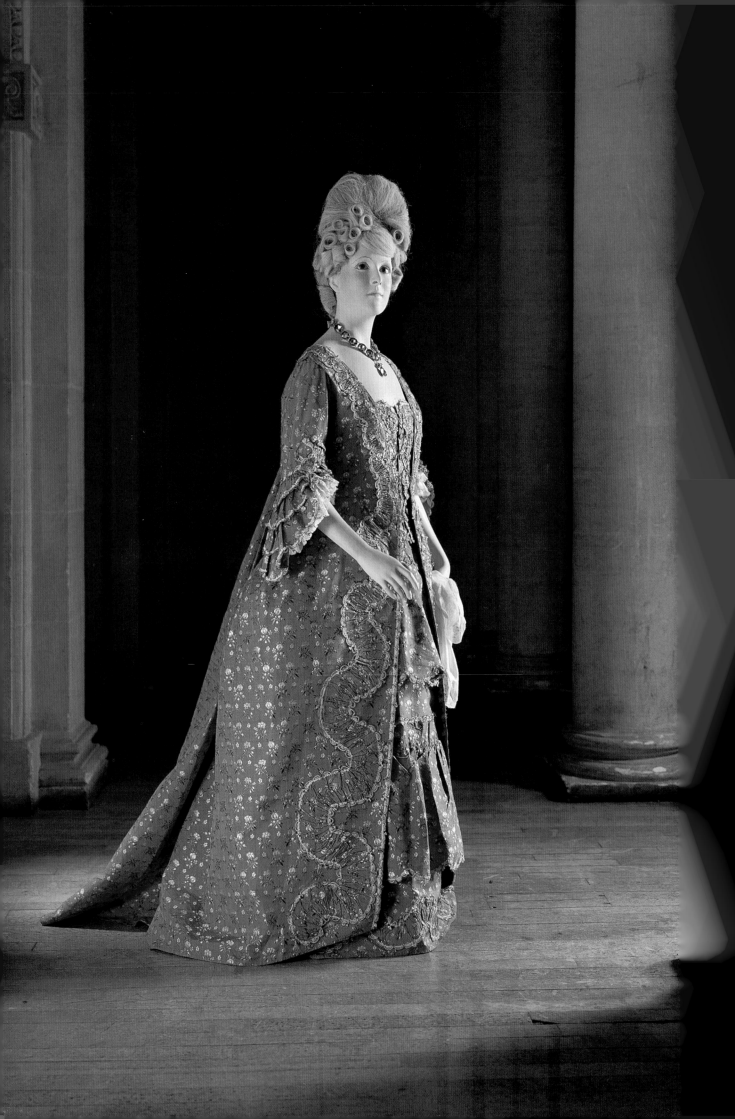

The Museum of Costume

'There is no difficulty in telling fashionable clothes from dowdy ones even when dealing with modes that have long since passed out of existence.'

Doris Langley Moore, 1963

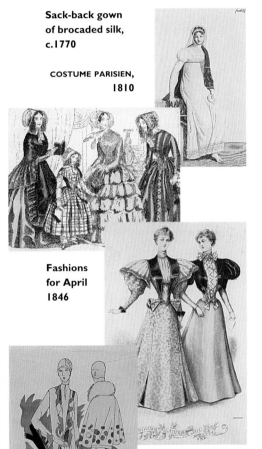

Sack-back gown of brocaded silk, c.1770

COSTUME PARISIEN, 1810

Fashions for April 1846

THE YOUNG LADIES JOURNAL, 1895

TRES PARISIEN, 1927

A Collection comes to Bath

The Museum of Costume was opened in the Assembly Rooms on 23 May 1963. It was the creation of Doris Langley Moore, a designer, collector and historian, who gave her famous private collection of costume to the city of Bath.

Over the next three decades the museum expanded to become one of the largest and finest collections of fashionable dress in this country. Mrs Moore had an unerring eye for quality and style; her experience in the theatre also contributed to the imaginative flair and liveliness of her displays.

These are traditions the Museum of Costume has sought to continue since Doris Langley Moore's retirement in 1974.

Note: The extensive displays are changed regularly so items illustrated in this guide may not be on view at the time of a visit to the museum.

The Story of Fashion

This is a museum of fashionable clothes. The displays illustrate the changing styles of dress for men, women and children over the last 400 years. The earliest pieces date from the 1580s-90s, the late Elizabethan period. The most recent are the fashions of today. Through the unique Dress of the Year scheme a new outfit is added to the collection each year to keep it up to date. Old or new, every item is an original costume.

Eighteenth-century silk dresses hanging in store
The museum has a large collection with only a proportion on display at a time. This allows exhibits to be changed regularly and the costumes to 'rest'. Dresses are stored on padded coathangers or boxed, with acid-free tissue paper.

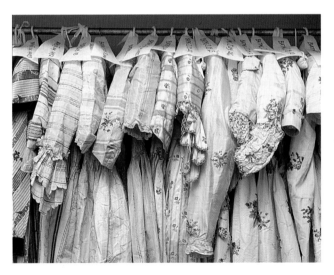

The fashionable silhouette

By emphasising natural contours or trying to disguise them, clothes can create a fashionable silhouette. These fashion plates show how the waistline can be set at different levels, be made to look smaller by enlarging the hips or shoulders, or made to disappear. Fashion is an endlessly evolving process. Every new style has evolved from one already established. Fashion itself consists of new or different ways of presenting the human figure.

The Exhibition Gallery
In addition to the chronological displays in the museum, there are also regular exhibitions that highlight a particular aspect of fashion.

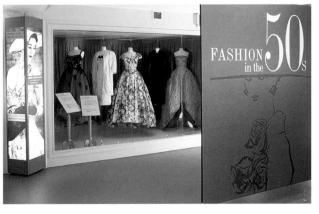

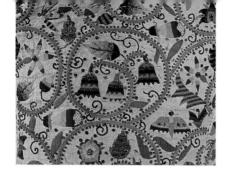

Early Treasures

'... wrought all over from the gartering place upward, with needle worke, clogged with silke of all colours, with byrdes, foules, beastes and antiques portraited all over sumptuous sorte.'

Philip Stubbes 1583

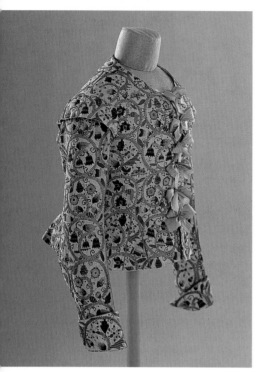

Woman's jacket, c.1620

Linen, embroidered with coloured silks, silver and silver gilt thread and spangles. The jacket fastens with bows of salmon pink silk ribbon. The silks retain much of their original brilliant colour. Only natural dyes were used at this date and all sewing was done by hand.

Two early seventeenth century gloves

These buff leather gloves with embroidered gauntlets date from around 1600-25. They come from the Spence Collection on loan from the Worshipful Company of Glovers of London.

Elizabethan and Jacobean

The earliest garments in the museum's collection date from the reigns of Elizabeth I (1558-1603) and James I (1603-1625). Because of the fragile nature of textiles they are rare survivals. These are not complete costumes but individual pieces which were preserved for their embroidery.

Linen underclothes (a man's shirt and woman's shift or chemise) could be as beautifully decorated as outer garments such as jackets, caps and gloves. Embroidery of this period was extremely skilful and England became famous for its blackwork in particular. Coloured silks, gold and silver thread and spangles were also used to create patterns of flowers, insects and animals.

From Cloth to Clothing

At this period all garments were made of cloth woven from natural fibres. It was not until the end of the nineteenth century that the first artificial silk was produced, while other modern man-made fibres date from the twentieth century.

The four natural fibres used for clothing were wool, silk, linen and cotton. Wool and silk derive from animals and were mainly used for outer garments. Linen and cotton are vegetable fibres and have been widely used for underclothing. Cotton, however, did not become fashionable in European dress until the late seventeenth century.

Gloves

Although gloves for everyday use could be quite plain, very decorative examples were made for special occasions. Gauntlet gloves were richly embroidered, usually on a separate, deep cuff of stiffened silk which was joined at the wrist. The seam was disguised by a ruffle of silk ribbon and metallic lace or braid. The cuffs flared and were left open on one side with silk ribbon gussets. This prevented the glove from crushing the lace cuffs of a man's doublet or woman's bodice. Very long, narrow fingers were a fashionable feature.

The Museum of Costume has a very fine collection of early decorative gloves on loan from the Worshipful Company of Glovers of London. The Spence Collection numbers over 100 pairs from the early seventeenth century to the mid nineteenth century.

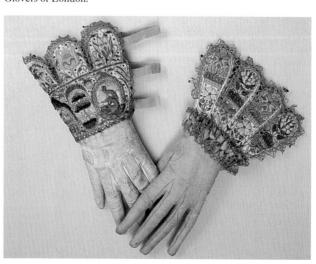

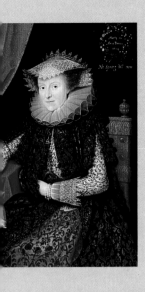

Lady Scudamore by M. Gheeraerts the younger, 1614-15
This portrait shows an embroidered linen jacket worn with a contrasting skirt and overgown. She wears a plain, starched ruff and lace cuffs to match her cap. Her gloves are plain.

Man's shirt, c.1580-90 and Woman's shift, c.1610
Both made of linen, these were the basic undergarments of the period. It was usual to decorate the parts which might be visible – at the front, neck and wrists. Embroidery was not only decorative. It could strengthen the areas exposed to wear and disguise soiling.

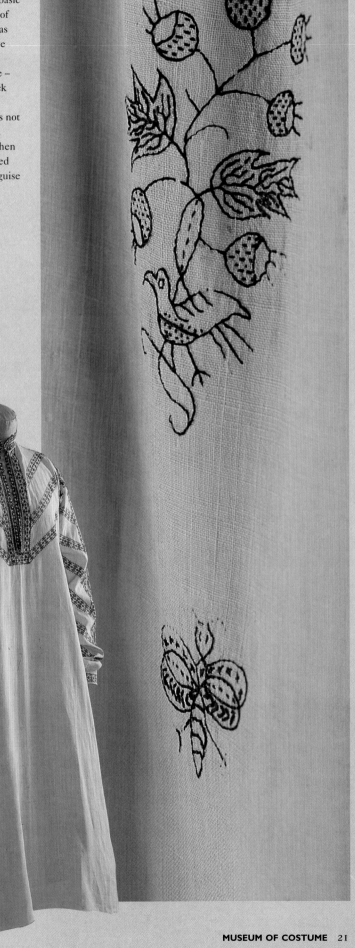

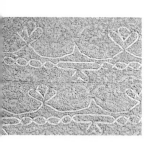

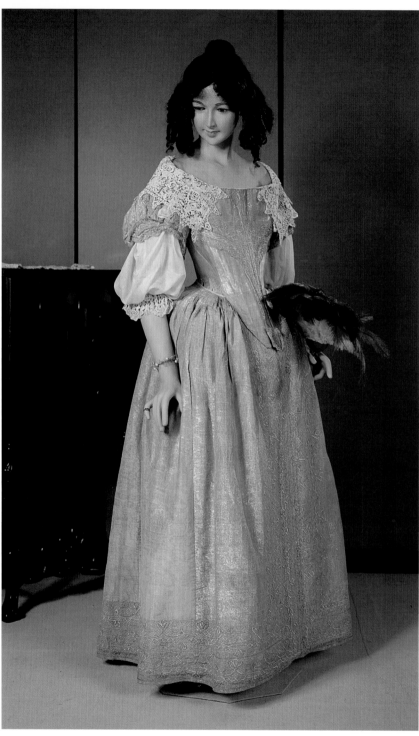

Dress (bodice and skirt) of silver tissue trimmed with cream parchment lace, c.1660
The lace collar is of a similar date.

Restoration Fashion

With the Restoration of the Monarchy in 1660 English fashion became more decorative and colourful. After the Civil War and Commonwealth of the mid seventeenth century, Charles II's court was lively and social. The diarist Samuel Pepys has left many descriptions of clothes, telling us that the king himself started a new fashion. In 1666 he began wearing a 'vest' beneath a knee-length indoor coat. By 1670 the earliest form of the three-piece suit was established, consisting of coat, waistcoat and knee breeches.

The Silver Tissue Dress

The museum's earliest complete costume dates from about 1660. This dress is a rare survival and in remarkable condition. The separate bodice and skirt are made of a fine cream silk woven with silver thread. It is trimmed with handmade lace. The boned bodice has a wide neckline, short sleeves and a long waist dipping to a point at the centre front. The full, round skirt is finely pleated over the hips.

This is a formal dress and fine enough to have been worn at Court.

Ribbons

Ribbons were a popular form of decoration in the later seventeenth century. Bunches of ribbon loops, knots, bows and rosettes were worn by both men and women. At the height of the fashion men could wear ribbons on the shoulder, at the waist and the knees. Ribbons were even used to decorate the bathing dresses and caps worn in the baths at Bath.

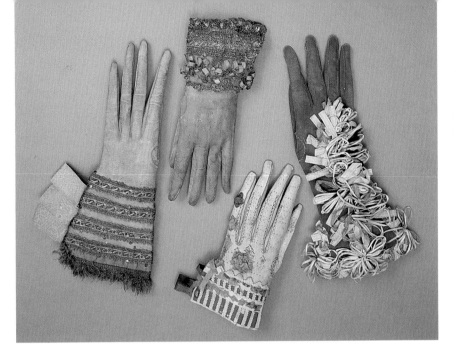

Gloves trimmed with ribbons, 1630s-1680s
Coloured silk ribbons have been fancifully looped, applied to or threaded through the leather to create three-dimensional effects.

'... a strange effeminate age when men strive to imitate women in their apparell, viz long periwigs, patches in their faces, painting, short wide breeches like petticotes, muffs and their clothes highly scented, bedecked with ribbons of all colours.'

Anthony Wood, 1663

Detail of the King's Bath by Thomas Johnson, 1675
Johnson's figures illustrate the new three-piece suit for men in the 1670s. Ribbon trimming on the knee breeches (and the lady's sleeves) can just be seen.

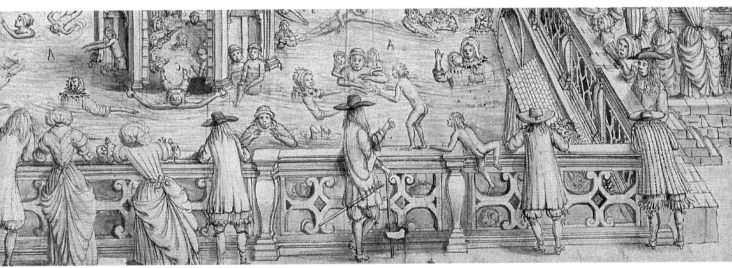

'The Ladyes goes into the Bath with Garments made of a fine yellow canvas, which is stiff and made large with great sleeves like a parson's gown; the water fills it up so that its borne off that your shape is not seen ...
The Gentlemen have drawers and wastcotes of the same sort of canvas, this is the best linen, for the bath water will Change any other yellow.'

Celia Fiennes 1687

For bathing at this date women wore caps and shifts of yellow linen trimmed with black ribbons. Gentlemen wore knee-length drawers of linen but young children could bathe naked. No bathing garments of this period have survived so this drawing provides valuable information about spa dress.

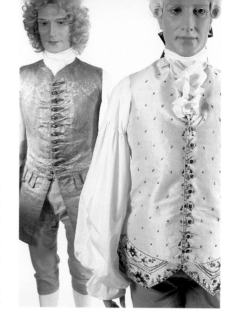

The Full Bottomed Wig

Long hair for men became fashionable in the mid seventeenth century and by the 1660s wigs were worn (Samuel Pepys bought his first in 1663). In the eighteenth century this was a universal fashion and styles changed frequently. Until about 1710 the full bottomed wig was usual – a long, curled wig with a centre parting. Later styles were shorter and lighter and on formal occasions the wig was greased and powdered. Men cut or shaved their own hair to give the wig a close fit.

A Rich Suit of Clothes

A three-piece suit of coat, waistcoat and knee breeches of wool or silk was worn over a linen shirt, drawers and knitted silk stockings. The finest coats and waistcoats could be lavishly embroidered and also trimmed with gold and silver lace.

A particularly fine example of about 1720 is the coat with matching stockings (right) made for a young Scottish nobleman, Sir Thomas Kirkpatrick. The brown wool coat is embroidered on the front, back and sleeves in silver and silver gilt thread.

Mens' waistcoats

A waistcoat was an essential part of the fashionable three-piece suit for men throughout the eighteenth century. Waistcoats were frequently made of woven silk and professionally embroidered by hand in coloured silk threads.

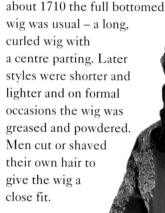

Man's formal coat, c.1720

This is an example of West Country broadcloth, the finest woollen cloth of this date, although the coat was probably tailored in London. It is a coat for very formal or Court wear. Deep vents in the side and back seams allowed the sword to pass through. Typical of the early eighteenth century Baroque taste, this sophisticated embroidery would have been carried out in a professional workshop. The design includes stylised carnations, pomegranates, and other floral ornaments, asymmetric fan motifs and scaled 'S' scrolls.

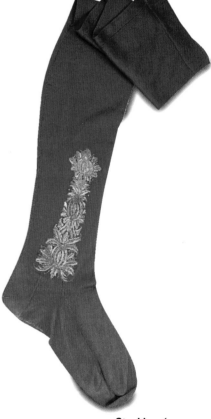

Stocking, (one of a pair) c.1720

The original stockings to match this coat are made of brown, machine-knitted silk with silver embroidery. The bands of decoration are known as 'clocks'.

**Fan leaf detail,
c.1737**

This view of the
interior of the Pump
Room includes
Richard 'Beau'
Nash, the Master of
Ceremonies. By the
1730s men's wigs
were shorter and
flatter on the crown.
Women's skirts were
full and bell-shaped.
Straw hats over
white caps and long
aprons were usual
for outdoor, morning
wear.

Undress Wear

Indoors at home, on informal
occasions, gentlemen could relax
by removing their wigs and coats.
These were replaced by a soft cap,
called a night cap or morning cap
and a loose gown. This was known
by a variety of names such as
dressing gown, night gown, morning
gown or India gown, but all refer to
a unfitted garment not unlike a
modern dressing gown.

The Master of Ceremonies,
Richard Nash disapproved of these
informal garments in the Pump
Room at Bath. His Rules for Polite
Behaviour of 1742 stated '*that
Gentlemen of Fashion never appearing
in a morning before the Ladies in
Gowns and Caps shew Breeding and
Respect.*'

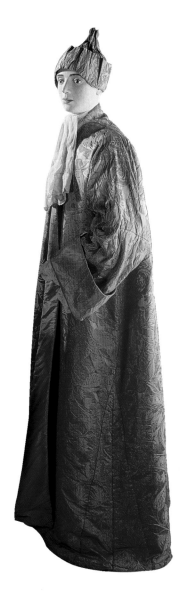

**Dressing gown
and cap of pink
silk damask,
c.1720**

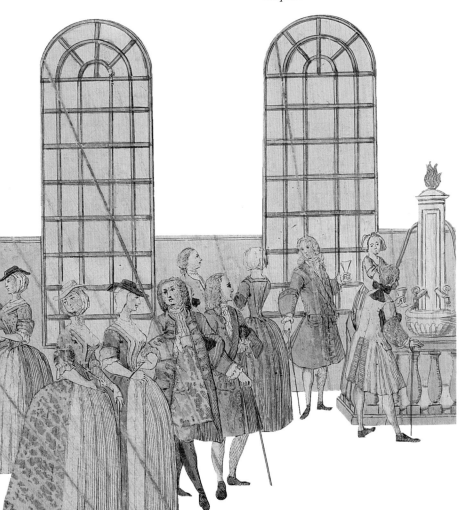

*'Being His Majesty's
birthday, Nash gave a ball
at Lyndsey's Rooms; he wore
his gold laced clothes on the
occasion and looked so fine
that, standing by chance in
the middle of the dancers,
he was taken by many at a
distance for a gilt garland.'*

Lord Chesterfield 1734

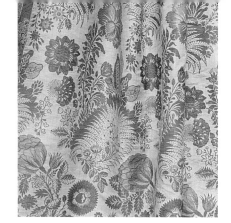

Women's Fashions: 1740s-1770s

Town and Country

For daytime wear in town or in the country, the well-dressed woman would wear a silk dress. There were several different styles of gown. Some were open at the front, worn over an underskirt or 'petticoat' which could either match or contrast with the gown. The opening between the front edges of the bodice was filled in by a stiffened triangular panel called a stomacher.

Light scarves or 'neck handkerchiefs' were often worn to cover the neck and shoulders. Aprons were another fashionable eighteenth-century accessory. They were intended to be decorative rather than practical but were not correct with evening dress. Caps were worn indoors and wide-brimmed straw hats out of doors, in the garden or country. Shoes were often made in fabric to match the dress but had leather soles. Both men's and women's shoes fastened with buckles which secured two straps overlapping the instep.

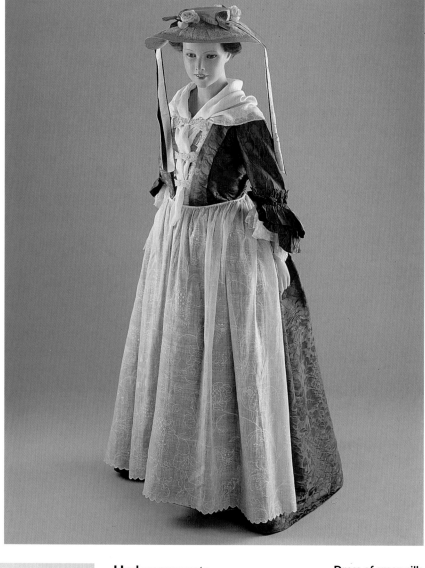

Pair of stays, c.1775

The corset was worn over the shift (never next to the skin). In the eighteenth century it had shoulder straps and was laced at the back. Made of stout linen or cotton, the corset was stiffened with whalebone. A rigid 'busk' of wood, horn or ivory was inserted at the centre front to keep it rigid.

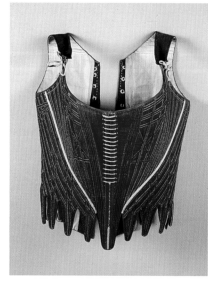

Undergarments

Beneath the gown a long, sleeved shift of linen, a pair of stays (corset) and a hoop petticoat were worn. Stout linen petticoats reinforced with cane hoops gave the skirt its fashionable bell shape until the 1730s; the skirt then flattened at the front and back and extended at the sides to become almost rectangular in the 1740s. Stockings of knitted silk or cotton were held up by garters.

Dress of green silk damask, 1747

The silk has been identified as a design by Anna Maria Garthwaite, woven at Spitalfields in London. England had a small silk industry but the finest European silks were made in France and Italy. The neck handkerchief and long apron are of white embroidered muslin.

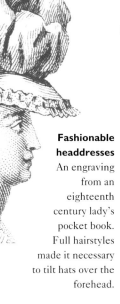

'*I was extremely diverted, last ball-night, to see the Master of the Ceremonies leading, with great solemnity, to the upper-end of the room, an antiquated Abigail, dressed in her lady's cast clothes; whom he (I suppose) mistook for some countess just arrived at the Bath.*'

TOBIAS SMOLLETT 1771

Fashionable headdresses
An engraving from an eighteenth century lady's pocket book. Full hairstyles made it necessary to tilt hats over the forehead.

Detail, dress silk (above left)
Brocade, c.1740

Brocaded silk dresses and man's suit of cut velvet, 1760s-70s
The distinctive back of the sack dress is illustrated on the left. By the 1770s women's hair styles were fashionably high and full.

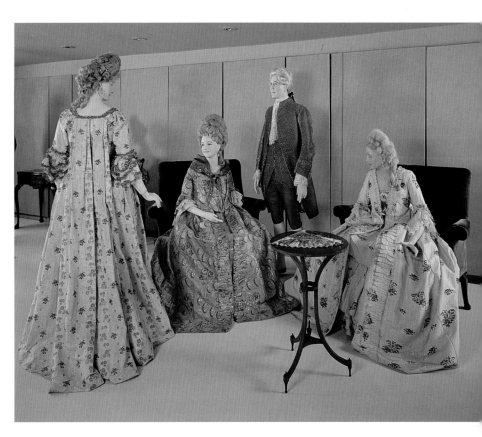

The Sack

Perhaps the most popular style of women's dress in the eighteenth century was the sack-back gown, fashionable until the 1770s. Its distinctive feature was a loose back falling straight from the shoulders in two double box pleats. When made for more formal occasions the back could be lengthened into a short train and the gown was extensively trimmed (often with gold or silver lace). Sometimes the skirt was looped up and draped over the hips in the *polonaise* style.

Hair

During the first half of the century women's hair was dressed close to the head and looked very neat. By the 1760s styles were looser and fuller, becoming extremely tall in the 1770s. Hair was greased, powdered and arranged over pads to achieve this effect. The most elaborate arrangements were intended for formal, evening occasions.

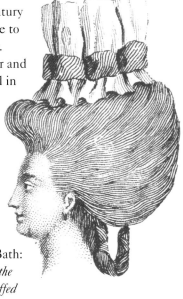

The heroine of Smollett's novel HUMPHRY CLINKER (1771) wrote to a friend from Bath: '*I was not above six hours under the hands of the hair-dresser, who stuffed my head with as much black wool as would have made a quilted petticoat; and after all, it was the smallest head in the assembly, except my aunt's.*'

Courtly Splendour

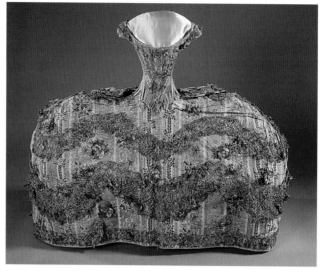

Dress for Court Wear

Many of the clothes which survive in museums today are garments which were worn for special occasions. They were treasured and kept in families because they were particularly fine or expensive. This often happened with court dress, for both men and women.

In the eighteenth century it was customary for leading members of society to attend court occasions and pay their respects to the monarch (for example on the King's or Queen's birthday). The most formal and splendid clothes were expected at these functions. New clothes were made of the finest silks, embellished with woven patterns or covered with embroidery. Metallic thread, lace and spangles added richness and sparkle when worn in candlelight.

Hoop Petticoats

The very wide hoop petticoats fashionable in the 1740s remained usual for court wear long after they passed out of everyday fashion. This was because court dress was extremely formal and tended not to alter quickly (another feature of court dresses was a long train).

'Hoop petticoat' is a general term for several different types of support. These ranged from round or fan-shaped petticoats distended by cane hoops to oblong arrangements and side hoops – rather like baskets or 'paniers' worn over each hip. These supports exaggerated the width of the skirt but were more flexible than they might appear.

A Fashion Doll's Court Dress

Before the regular publication of fashion journals and illustrations towards the end of the eighteenth century, new styles of dress were often shown in miniature. A dressmaker might have a series of fashion dolls dressed in the latest fashions to show to clients.

A very rare example is a fashion doll's court dress of about 1770. It shows an unusual style of English court dress and consists of a stiffened bodice, wide skirt and separate train of brocaded silk trimmed with silver lace.

Fashion doll's dress, c.1770
The dress is in three parts: short-sleeved, boned bodice or 'corset', skirt or 'petticoat' and a train. The silk is French, woven with silver and yellow stripes interspersed with knots of pink and yellow roses. This was probably made by a dressmaker to demonstrate a particular style of court dress to the royal family. The original doll no longer survives.

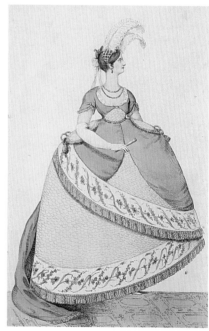

'A Lady of Quality in the Birthday Court Dress' 1808.
This fashion plate published in La Belle Assemblée magazine shows hoops still being worn in the early nineteenth century. They remained usual for court wear until 1820.

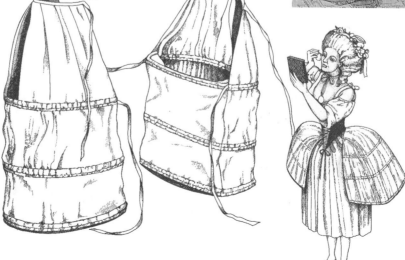

'After much persuasion and many debates within myself I consented to go with Lady Dysart to the Prince's birthday, humbly drest in my pink damask, white and gold handkerchief, plain green ribbon and Lady Sunderland's buckles for my stays ... I never saw so much finery without any mixture of trumpery in my life.'

Mary Delany 1738

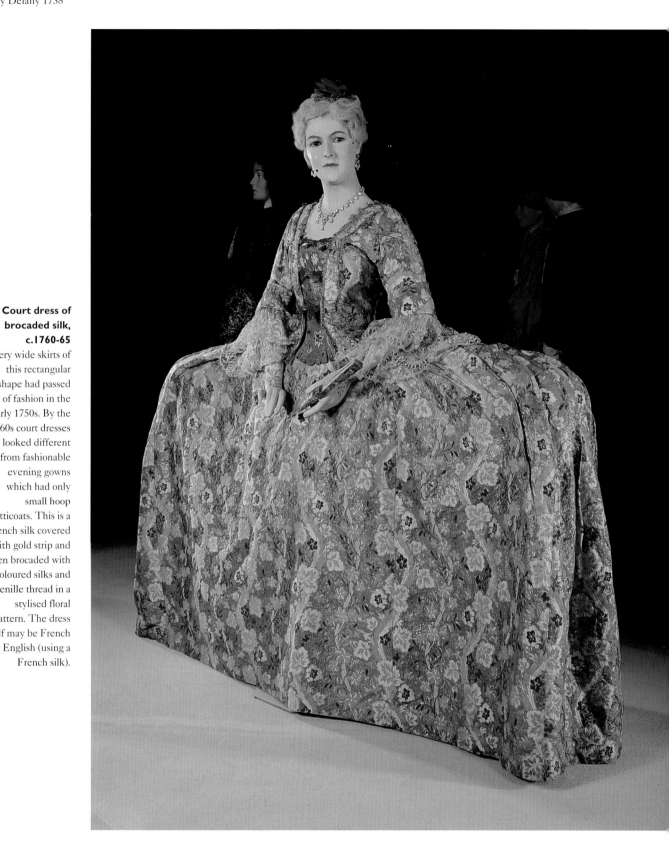

Court dress of brocaded silk, c.1760-65
Very wide skirts of this rectangular shape had passed out of fashion in the early 1750s. By the 1760s court dresses looked different from fashionable evening gowns which had only small hoop petticoats. This is a French silk covered with gold strip and then brocaded with coloured silks and chenille thread in a stylised floral pattern. The dress itself may be French or English (using a French silk).

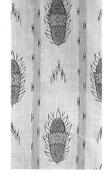

Late Eighteenth Century

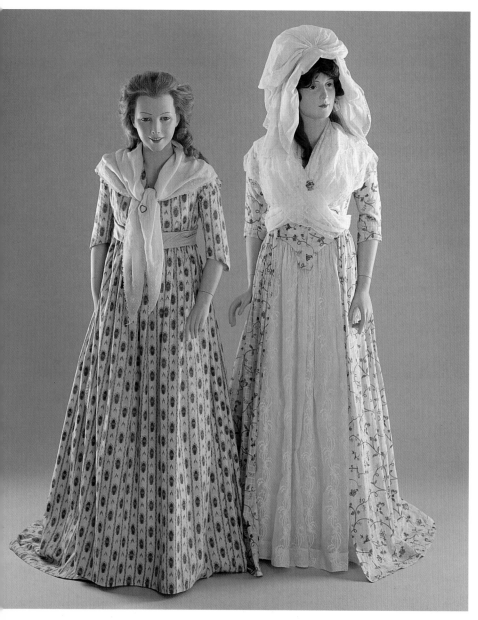

A New Mood

The 1780s and 1790s saw a complete change in mood and the emergence of new styles of dress for both men and women. The taste for rich and formal clothes gave way to a liking for simpler, more practical garments.

This was, in part, a response to social and political changes. Following the outbreak of the French Revolution in 1789, for example, anything which appeared aristocratic or ostentatious went out of favour. Men began to discard lace wrist ruffles, jewelled shoe buckles and powdered wigs. A plainer form of dress was adopted for daytime wear, using woollen cloth in sober colours for coats and breeches. For women, the light-weight cottons and linens now being imported from the East were becoming fashionable and the softer texture of these materials affected the cut and shape of the gown.

In the arts there was a new mood of romanticism in the late eighteenth century. A renewed interest in the natural world, in the imaginative and the picturesque encouraged a liking for easy and informal clothes. Country wear, especially men's riding dress, began to be worn in town.

Printed cotton dresses, 1780s-90s
On the left is an example of the new one-piece gown which was replacing the older form (right) of an open-fronted gown with underskirt or 'petticoat'.
The petticoat, neck handkerchief and cap on the right are of white embroidered muslin.

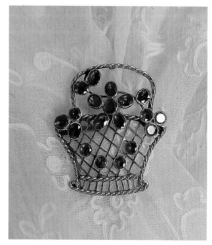

Detail, brooch, 1780s-90s
This garnet and gold basket brooch, reflecting the late-eighteenth century interest in the countryside, is pinned to a neck handkerchief of white embroidered muslin.

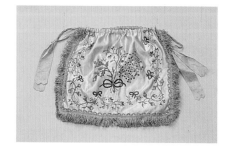

Embroidered bag, late eighteenth century
A drawstring bag of cream satin embroidered with coloured silks and trimmed with pink silk fringe.

'an English chintz, three yards ell-wide. Thirteen shillings, June 1781'

BARBARA JOHNSON'S ALBUM

A Changing Line in Dress

Although silks were still worn the preference was for materials in lighter colours and textures with delicate patterns. By day, the printed linens (chintzes) and cotton fabrics such as Indian muslin were increasingly used for women's dresses. Muslins could be plain, printed, embroidered or woven with a small design.

A slimmer and more fluid silhouette emerged as the waistline began to rise and skirts were more softly pleated and draped. Cross-over bodices or bodices filled in with a white muslin neck handkerchief were particularly fashionable by the 1790s.

Fashion plate for April 1797

From THE GALLERY OF FASHION published by Niklaus von Heideloff from 1794 to 1803. This was the first English magazine devoted entirely to fashion and the first to be issued with all its plates in colour. The engraved plates were hand-coloured aquatints. This lively illustration shows ladies in outdoor dress. Bonnets, shawls, long gloves and large fur muffs helped to keep them warm.

'The Caricature Dance Fan for 1794'

Inexpensive fans with printed paper leaves and plain wooden sticks could be bought or given away as souvenirs. Fans of this kind would have been used in the Bath Assembly Rooms.

Hair and Hats

In the 1780s the towering hair arrangements gradually subsided into a mass of loose curls which tumbled onto the shoulders. This gave women a more natural and romantic appearance although caps needed to be large enough to accommodate the size of the head. Broad-brimmed hats trimmed with flowers or feathers were fashionable accessories and are often seen in paintings of this date by Thomas Gainsborough.

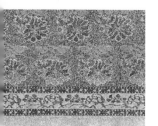

Regency Style

The early nineteenth century is usually associated with the Regency style although to be precise, the Regency period only lasted from 1811 to 1820. In 1811 George III became permanently insane and his son, the Prince of Wales, became Regent. After his father's death in 1820 the Prince Regent was crowned George IV.

Neo-Classical Taste

A distinctive style of female dress had evolved by 1800. Very short-waisted gowns with long flowing skirts, often made of white muslin, were fashionable for over a decade. For evening wear the neckline was cut low and sleeves were short. In the daytime however, dresses were high to the neck with long sleeves. White was especially fashionable but other colours could be worn.

These simple, light gowns were inspired by the neo-classical taste and were intended to imitate the draperies of ancient Greek and Roman statues. Muslin was an ideal dress fabric because it was soft and almost transparent, gently outlining the natural contours of the figure. It could also be washed easily (unlike silk) which made the fashion for white possible.

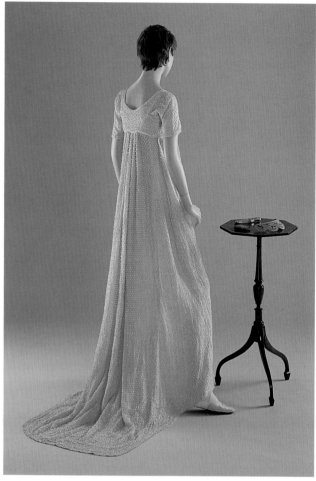

Evening dress c.1804

This one-piece dress is made of white muslin embroidered all over with white beads. Additional fabric was pleated into the centre back to create a small train and to allow the skirt to drape gently round the legs.

The Pump Room, Bath by J. C. Nattes, 1804

This contemporary print illustrates the neo-classical taste in both architecture and dress. By 1800 fashionable day dress for men was a smartened version of riding dress: tail coat, knee breeches, riding boots and top hat.

Printed glove, c.1800

White kid gloves with printed designs were a fashionable accessory to dress at this date.

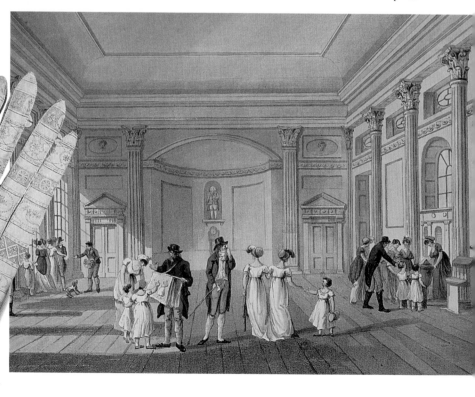

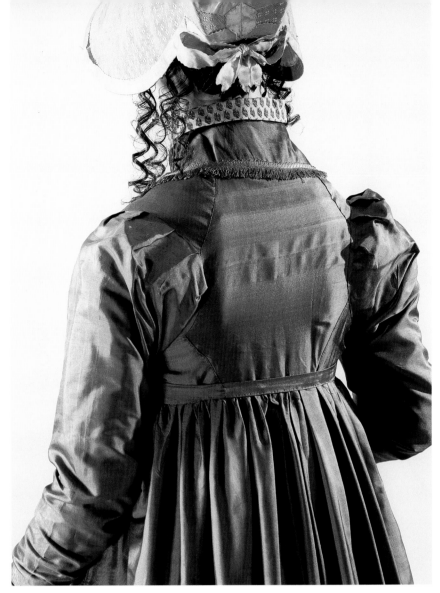

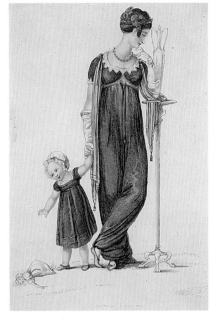

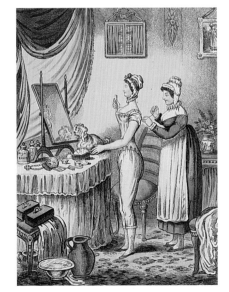

Lady's Toilette, 1810

A lady inserts a busk at the centre front of her corset while her maid, in a cap and dark gown, tightens the lacing at the back.

Undergarments

Corsets were still worn by conventional women but they became lighter and more flexible as dress styles changed. A white linen chemise was the main undergarment but in the first decades of the century long drawers began to be worn. Knitted silk or cotton stockings were held up by garters until the 1870s when suspenders were introduced.

Men's Dress

A three-piece suit remained standard wear for men although the coat and waistcoat worn with either breeches, pantaloons or trousers did not match at this date. In the evening a dark cloth tail coat was worn with a light waistcoat and cream or fawn breeches and white stockings. Trousers began to be adopted for informal daytime wear and were in general use by 1825.

Pelisse, c.1815

'Pelisse' was the early-nineteenth century term for this type of high-waisted coat. A pelisse was often made of soft twilled silk and was fashionable in Jane Austen's time.

Mourning dresses, 1809

Black was worn for mourning, by both adults and children. These dresses are of muslin.

Detail of shawl (above left)

Woven silk and cashmere, early nineteenth century.

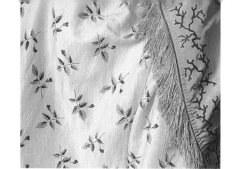

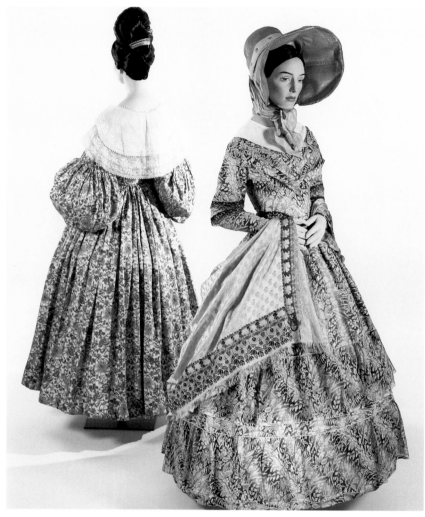

Fanciful Fashions

During the reigns of George IV (1820-1830) and his brother William IV (1830-1837) women's fashions were highly decorative. As the waistline dropped to its natural level skirts began to widen and sleeves were puffed out in the gigot or leg-of-mutton shape. To counterbalance the new width at the shoulder and hem, hair arrangements and headdresses were enlarged and embellished. Silks returned to fashion with the lifting of a ban on French imports in 1826. Bright, clear colours were set off by embroidery and lace.

A New Queen

The accession of the young Queen Victoria in June 1837 coincided with a change of mood and a quieter taste in dress. Enormous sleeves collapsed and then tightened, hair was more simply dressed and clothes looked demure. The 1840s favoured softer colours and plain or delicately patterned fabrics. Out of doors a modest appearance was emphasised by deep-brimmed 'poke' bonnets and enveloping shawls. At home, all married ladies wore indoor caps.

Hair

The 1830s saw some of the most elaborate hair styles of the nineteenth century. For the evening, hair was stiffened, looped and curled (with the aid of gum arabic or wire) into exaggerated shapes. The asymmetrical 'Apollo Knot' was a particularly fashionable arrangement. With the quieter 'Madonna' style the hair was smoothed flat from a centre parting. In the 1840s long, loose ringlets on either side of the face gave women a girlish appearance.

Day dresses, 1830s

The printed wool dress on the left shows the full gigot sleeves of the mid 1830s. The dress is worn with a white cotton embroidered pelerine collar. By the end of the decade, sleeves were much more closely fitting, as seen in the green and purple printed wool dress. The bonnet is made of finely plaited straw trimmed with a woven silk ribbon.

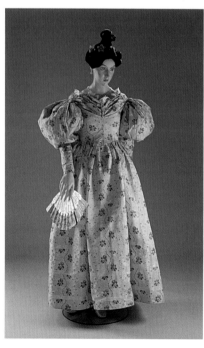

Brocaded silk dress, 1833

It was fashionable in the 1830s and 1840s to make dresses from eighteenth century silks. Sometimes the separate skirt was made with two bodices: one with a high neck and long sleeves for daytime wear and the other with a low neck and short sleeves for the evening.

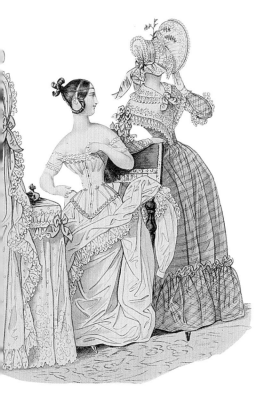

'Very young unmarried ladies, whom Fashion will not permit to dress expensively, wear organdy and tarlatane, very simply trimmed; while gauze, crape, satin, tulle and lace, all of the richest description and with splendid garnitures are adopted by married belles.'

LA BELLE ASSEMBLÉE, 1848

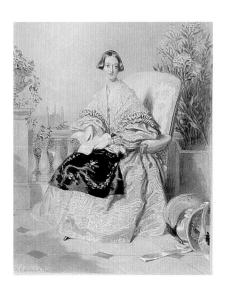

MODES DE PARIS, 1837
A fashionable corset (worn over a chemise of white linen or cotton) fastens at the front but is adjusted by tight lacing at the back. Full skirts also emphasised a slim waist and more underpetticoats were now worn.

Queen Victoria by A. E. Chalon, 1837-38
This portrait epitomises the new ideal of young womanhood in the late 1830s: pretty, modest and ladylike. Her dress is of moiré or watered silk, a very popular but expensive fabric, usually only worn by married women. Aprons, for decorative rather than practical use, were often worn at this time.

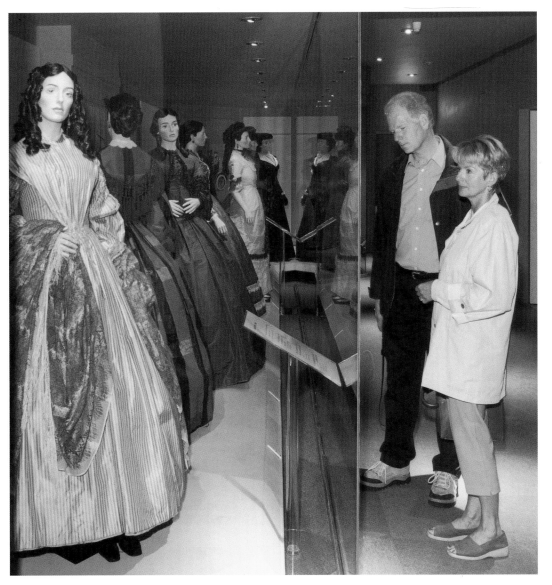

Day dress, 1840s
A striped dress in mauves and blues illustrates the taste for pastel colours and softly shimmering silk fabrics in the 1840s. It was fashionable to wear a large folded shawl as a warm garment in the open air. Lightweight woollen shawls were also worn indoors and their graceful drapery could enhance a dress.

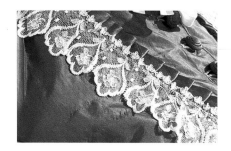

'Embroidery is used for all articles of ladies' dress: it cannot be too heavy or too rich:'

ILLUSTRATED LONDON NEWS, 1852

Mid Victorian Britain

As industry and trade expanded, the country's prosperity increased. New wealth and political reforms benefited the middle classes in particular. Fashion seemed to reflect this new confidence and the demand for consumer goods. Women's clothes were more opulent, making use of a wide range of materials and rich colours; skirts continued to expand, their width exaggerated by tiered flounces and crinoline petticoats.

The Business Suit

The middle-class businessman was a dominant element in Victorian society and the clothes he required were sober and sensible. Dark colours not only looked professional but were practical in dirty industrial cities. By the 1850s a black morning coat or frock coat with toning waistcoat and trousers were usual daytime wear, accompanied by a white shirt, dark silk neck tie, top hat and elastic-sided boots.

New Inventions

Fashion was affected by technological advances such as the invention of the sewing machine, paper patterns for home dressmaking, new chemical or 'aniline' dyes and the mass production of clothes. With a wider range of goods produced at cheaper prices, fashionable items came within the reach of the less well-off. Shopping patterns changed and the first department stores opened. Inexpensive railway travel (and the London Underground which started in 1863) made shops more accessible.

Crinoline, 1860s
The blue silk day dress is worn over petticoats and a crinoline frame. The dress (a separate bodice and skirt) is trimmed with 'blond' silk lace. The discovery of synthetic dyes encouraged a taste for stronger colours in the late 1850s and 1860s.

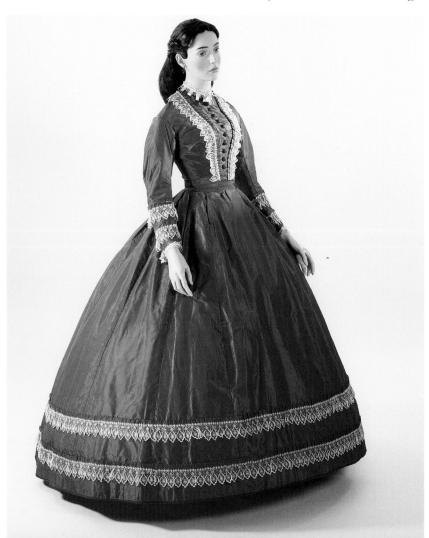

Advertisement, 1863
The crinoline changed its shape in the early 1860s, lengthening towards the back.

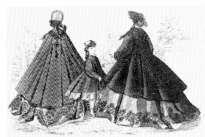

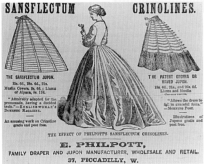

SANSFLECTUM CRINOLINES.

THE SANSFLECTUM JUPON.
11s. 6d., 18s. 6d., 21s.
Muslin Covers, 3s. 6d. ; Llama of Alpaca, 5s. 11d.

"Admirably adapted for the promenade, having a decided truth."—ENGLISH WOMAN'S DOMESTIC MAGAZINE.

An amusing work on Crinoline gratis and post free.

THE PATENT ONDINA OR WAVED JUPON.
19s. 6d., 21s., and 25s. 6d.
Llama and Muslin Covers.

"Allows the dress to fall in graceful folds."—MORNING POST.

Illustrations of Jupons gratis and post free.

THE EFFECT OF PHILPOTT'S SANSFLECTUM CRINOLINES.

E. PHILPOTT,
FAMILY DRAPER AND JUPON MANUFACTURER, WHOLESALE AND RETAIL.
37, PICCADILLY, W.

Advertisement, c.1865
Peter Robinson (which first opened in 1833) was one of the many fine dress shops to serve London customers. In the provinces, Jolly's of Bath (founded 1830) was one of the first of the new department stores.

Dress of printed wool muslin, late 1850s
Fashionable accessories for outdoor wear include the straw bonnet trimmed with silk ribbon, silk shawl and carriage parasol (with a folding ivory handle).

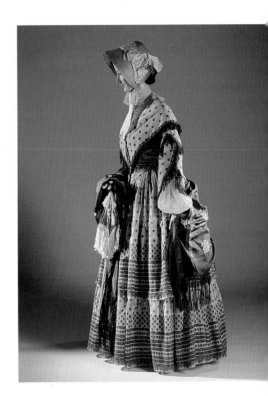

Dress of cream alpaca trimmed with blue silk, c.1872-3
The back-projecting fullness of the skirt is supported by a bustle.

Crinoline and Bustle

By 1856 the many layers of underpetticoats that held out the full skirt were replaced by one foundation garment : the crinoline frame. Made of graduated hoops of flexible steel, this cage-like petticoat created the perfect support for the ever-widening skirt and was light and easy to wear, though very impractical.

The crinoline passed out of fashion in the late 1860s, to be replaced by an alternative support: the bustle. Stiff frills of horsehair cloth or small wire frames exaggerated the fashionable fullness at the back of the skirt from around 1870 to 1876.

'Some ladies of the present day have returned to the old practice of wearing hoops to make the dresses stand out at the base ... who could imagine that there would be an attempt to revive the hoop petticoat in the nineteenth century?'

DRESS AS A FINE ART, 1854

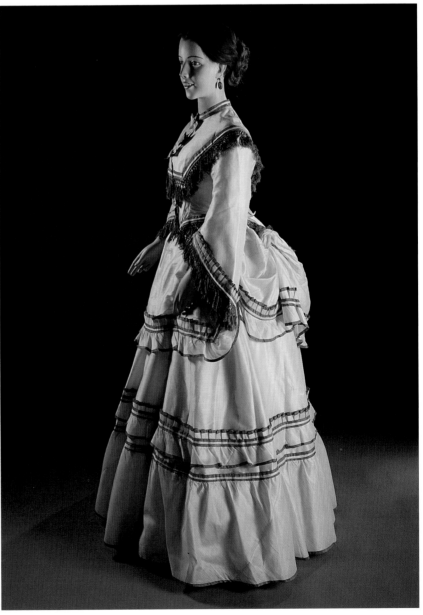

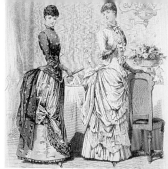

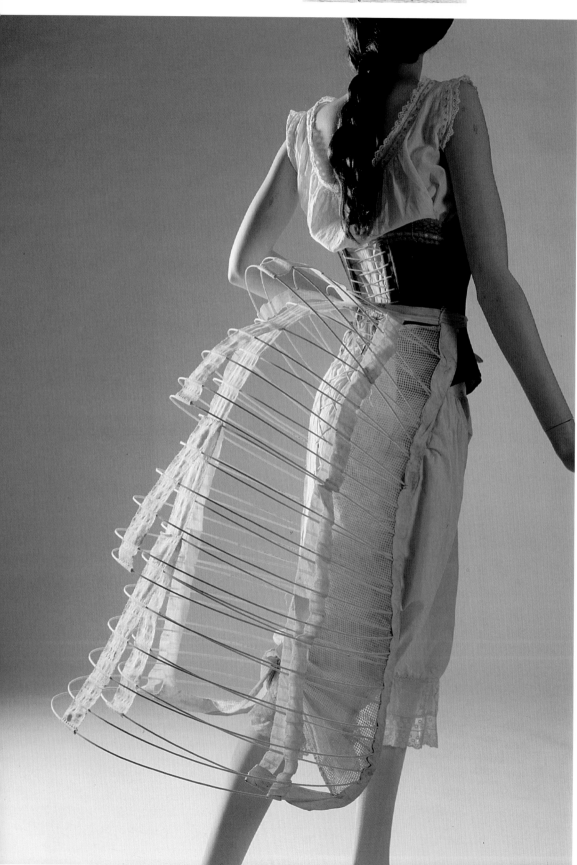

Fashions for 1884
A high neckband, long boned bodice and bustle skirt were typical of mid 1880s dress. The fringe, a new fashion in hair, was popularised by Princess Alexandra.

Thompson crinolette, c.1880
Worn with a chemise, corset and drawers.

A formal photograph, c.1895
This little girl can hardly move in her crisp cotton pinafore worn over a dress with large puffed sleeves.

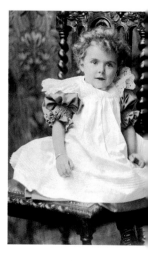

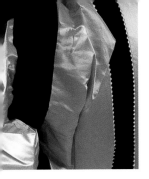

Late Victorian: 1875-1900

From Bustle to Crinolette

The bustle or 'dress improver', as it was sometimes called, passed out of fashion in the late 1870s. For a few years a tight and narrow line prevailed in dress but then the bustle returned: this time in a more exaggerated form. A more structural support was needed to give the skirt its projecting shape and the crinolette was adopted. As its name suggests, it looked like half a crinoline.

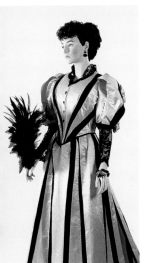

Dress of pink and black silk from *La Samaritaine*, a Paris department store, c.1893

1880s Opulence

Fashion in the 1880s favoured rich, dark colours and opulent fabrics. Although bodices were tight fitting, skirts were ample and heavily draped. Satins, velvets, brocades and bead-embroidered silks were worn in the evening.

For practical daytime wear a smart new type of dress was adopted by women: the tailor-made dress or matching coat and skirt in woollen cloth.

The 1890s saw a return of the leg-of-mutton sleeve, a flared A-line skirt and softer, fuller hairstyles.

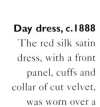

Day dress, c.1888
The red silk satin dress, with a front panel, cuffs and collar of cut velvet, was worn over a crinolette.

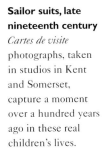

Sailor suits, late nineteenth century
Cartes de visite photographs, taken in studios in Kent and Somerset, capture a moment over a hundred years ago in these real children's lives.

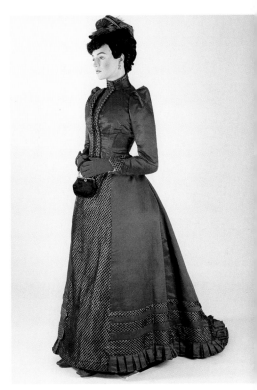

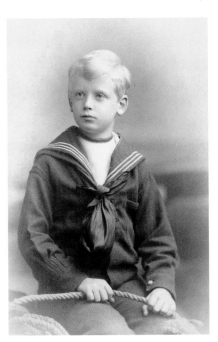

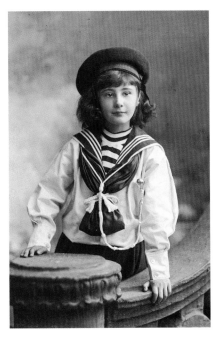

Children's Clothes

Victorian children's fashions followed adult styles. On formal occasions these could be elaborate and uncomfortable: stiffly-starched petticoats and white dresses, silk gowns with crinolines or bustles for little girls and velvet suits with lace collars for little boys.

By the end of the century, however, more practical and comfortable clothes were introduced. Sailor suits and knitted jerseys which began as informal, seaside wear became popular for both boys and girls.

It was usual for small boys to wear dresses until they were 'breeched' at the age of four or five.

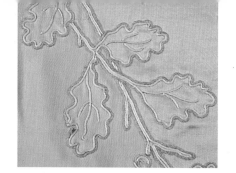

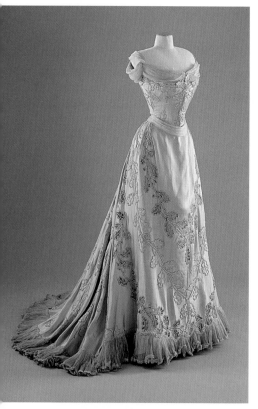

'He loved clothes and ... had so many he could never travel with less than two valets; and two more valets were left at home cleaning, brushing and pressing his vast wardrobe.'

Fleur Cowles, EDWARD VII AND HIS CIRCLE

Edwardian Elegance

The reign of Edward VII (1901-10) was an era of male and female elegance. With the King to set an example, British tailoring was at its height. Gentlemen wore frockcoats, starched collars, silk cravats and top hats for formal day wear although the more comfortable lounge suit was rapidly becoming popular.

Women's clothes were noted for their frou-frou quality: the audible rustle of petticoats and frothy trimmings of lace, ribbons and pintucks. The Art Nouveau taste encouraged a liking for pastel colours and sinuous curves.

First World War 1914-18

Although the war had a considerable effect on women's dress and social conventions, changes had begun some years earlier. The 1890s saw the emergence of the 'New Woman', young and independent, often working for her living. The suffrage movement was fighting hard for votes for women.

A gradual reaction against restricting forms of female dress resulted in simpler styles. By 1910 tightly-laced corsets were abandoned and in 1913 the hemline began to rise. War work made the shorter, wider skirt a virtual necessity by 1916. For some jobs trousers were required and for the first time they became acceptable wear for women.

Evening dress by Worth c.1902
This yellow silk dress trimmed with chiffon and inset embroidery was made for Lady Curzon when she was Vicereine of India. The curving lines of the bodice and trained skirt follow the fashionable S-bend shape.

Walking costume of natural silk, c.1900
Mannish fashions reflect the desire for a more active lifestyle and practical clothes for women.

Harrods, 1909
The line gradually straightened and narrowed after 1905. Extremely large hats were made popular by Lily Elsie in the 1909 operetta, THE MERRY WIDOW.

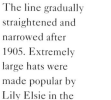

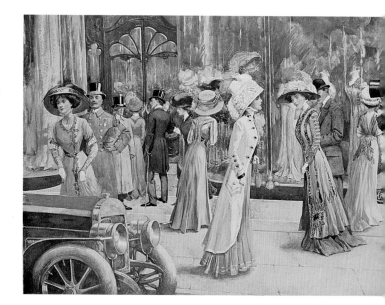

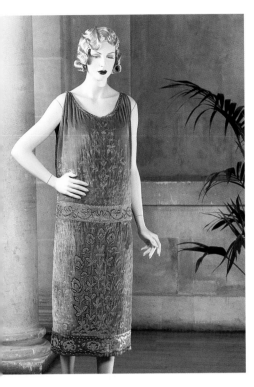

Dress designed by Callot Soeurs, c.1926
The Paris design house Callot Soeurs was famous for exquisitely embroidered evening dresses during the 1920s.

A Chanel suit, 1926
The French couturière, Coco Chanel, was famous for her casual but elegant jumper suits. This one is worn by the Ranee of Pudukota, a Society beauty of the 1920's and 1930's. A number of her clothes are in the Museum of Costume.

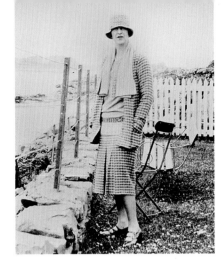

Twenties Style

The distinctive style of the 1920s is usually associated with the loose-fitting and drop-waisted dress with a short skirt. Until 1924, however, the skirt was quite long. It only reached knee level in 1927. The desirable figure was completely straight and foundation garments were made to flatten the bust and hips. Short hair was fashionable and cosmetics were more widely used. Evening bandeaux worn low over the forehead echoed the line of the deep-crowned cloche hat for daytime wear.

1920s clothes gave women a new freedom and ease of movement. It now became possible to be both comfortable and smart.

'To me the fashions of the twenties are infinitely alluring.'

Cecil Beaton, THE GLASS OF FASHION

Black hat with attached scarf by Agnès, 1920s
A soft, close fitting cloche hat was practical and stylish for the new sport of motoring.

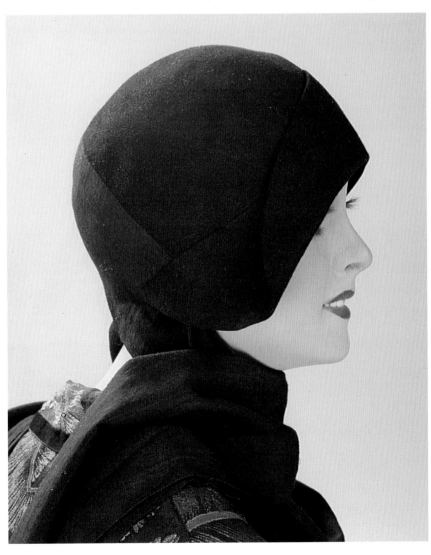

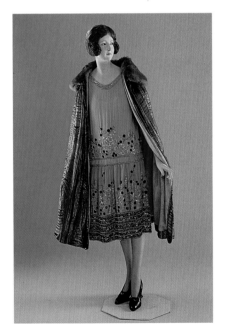

Beaded chiffon evening dress and lamé cape, late 1920s
Unshaped dresses relied on elaborate bead embroidery to give them interest and sparkle for evening wear.

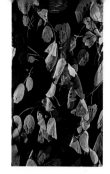

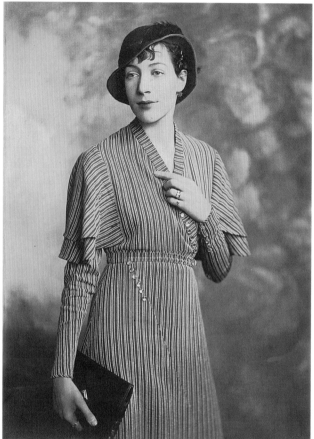

Bias Cut and Broad Shoulders

By 1930 there was a softer shape in women's dress. The natural contours of the bust, waist and hips were gently indicated and the skirt was lengthened. A more fluid line was created by cutting dress fabrics on the bias or cross-grain. This made them more pliable and easy to drape.

Later in the 1930s the shoulderline was accentuated, the waistline tightened and the hemline rose again.

Men's clothes grew looser and more comfortable in the inter-war years. Wide trousers (popularly known as 'Oxford Bags' in the mid 1920s) were balanced by squarer shoulders and easy fitting jackets.

Man's evening dress (white tie and tails) from THE TAILOR AND CUTTER, 1931
It was usual for men to dress in the evening. Fashionable suits were cut with wide lapels, a fitted waist and pleated trousers.

Doris Langley Moore (founder of the Museum of Costume) in the early 1930s. Photographed by Lafayette
This striped dress illustrates the streamlined effect of 1930s dress with its very neat accessories. Soft draping is achieved by the bias cut of her caped sleeves.

Dress design by Worth, 1936
The sunburst brooch was a favourite motif of the 1930s.

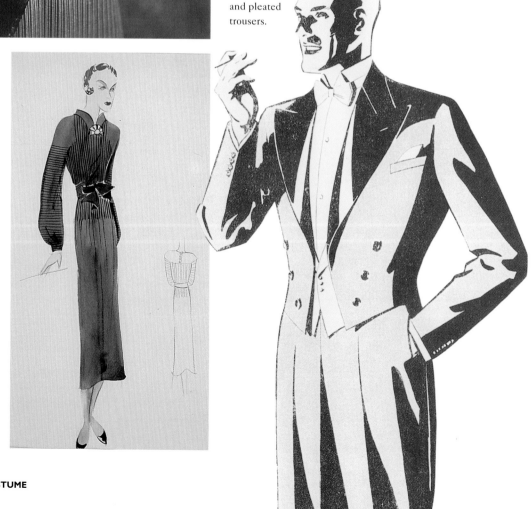

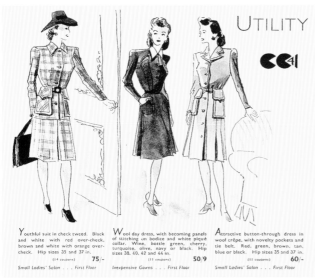

UTILITY

CC41

Youthful suit in check tweed. Black and white with red over-check, brown and white with orange over-check. Hip sizes 35 and 37 in.
(14 coupons) **75/-**
Small Ladies' Salon . . . First Floor

Wool day dress, with becoming panels of stitching on bodice and white piqué collar. Wine, bottle green, cherry, turquoise, olive, navy or black. Hip sizes 38, 40, 42 and 44 in.
(11 coupons) **50/9**
Inexpensive Gowns . . . First Floor

Attractive button-through dress in wool crêpe, with novelty pockets and tie belt. Red, green, brown, tan, blue or black. Hip sizes 35 and 37 in.
(11 coupons) **60/-**
Small Ladies' Salon . . . First Floor

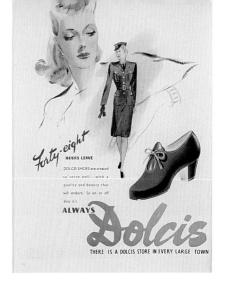

Utility mark, Harvey Nichols Catalogue, 1942

Advertisement, 1944
Sensible footwear was essential for war work. The mannish effect of uniforms was softened by wearing the hair long and elaborately curled.

The New Look
Once the war was over the fashion industry gradually revived. A general reaction against war-time austerity and a desire for luxury and femininity resulted in a 'New Look' – best expressed and summed up by Christian Dior's sensational Spring Collection for 1947. This new French designer created an alternative silhouette: long, full skirts, softly-rounded shoulders, tiny waists and very pretty high-heeled shoes. Other designers quickly followed suit and the New Look became universal.

Second World War: 1939-45
British fashion came to a virtual standstill with the outbreak of war. The need to economise on cloth and other materials resulted in clothes rationing (1941) and the utility scheme which from 1942 strictly governed the design and production of cloth and clothing. This left little scope for new styles or shapes. Thus the boxy suits with square shoulders and short skirts of the late 1930s remained in fashion until the end of hostilities.

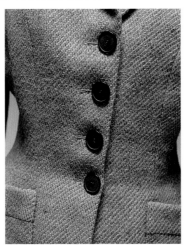

MAKE DO AND MEND

BOARD OF TRADE CAMPAIGN, 1943

'With one collection he had achieved an end to which all dress designers aspire, that of, overnight, making every woman wish she were naked with a chequebook.'

Ernestine Carter on Christian Dior

New Look suits, 1940s
The black suit comes from Christian Dior's original New Look collection of 1947 (and was worn by the ballerina Dame Margot Fonteyn).

The checked suit is by Balenciaga and has the alternative straight skirt. Detail of a tweed suit above.

Detail, 1930s dress (above left)

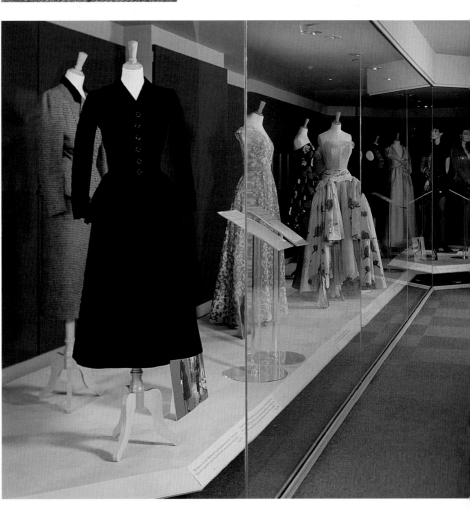

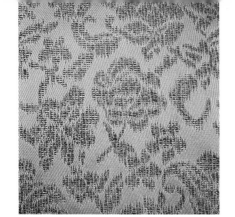

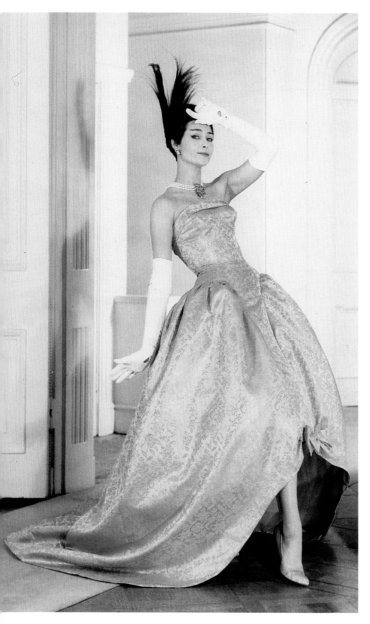

Ball dress of pink acetate and lurex brocade by John Cavanagh, 1958. This dress is in the museum's collection. Fashion models of the 1950s were noted for their poised but haughty expressions. The new man-made materials were welcomed with enthusiasm but designers later found they lacked the beauty and draping qualities of natural fibres.

Fifties Feminity

The New Look continued to dominate women's fashions in the early 1950s. Clothes followed the natural figure line and were neat, pretty and feminine. Accessories were carefully chosen – hats and gloves were still worn and matched shoes and bags. Grooming was important, with well-dressed hair and perfect makeup.

In the later fifties shapes became more artificial as the waistline moved and skirts ballooned out. Trousers and separates for casual wear were becoming more popular.

Man-made Fibres and Mass Production

Although artificial silk (rayon) was introduced at the beginning of this century and nylon in 1938, the widespread adoption of man-made fibres dates from the post war period. A number of other synthetic fibres such as acrylics, viscoses and polyesters (called by various names) have been produced. These have been used on their own to produce completely new fabrics or blended with natural fibres which are now relatively expensive.

Technical advances and improvements in sizing have resulted in the manufacture of well made and well fitting garments at reasonable prices. Ready made clothes have replaced made to measure for the majority of people since the 1950s.

'In terms of English teenagers, Teddy Boys were the start of everything ...'

Nik Cohn, TODAY THERE ARE NO GENTLEMEN (1971)

'The London Look has joined whisky and cashmere, pop groups and Carnaby Street as the latest rave wave around the world.'
Vogue, 1965

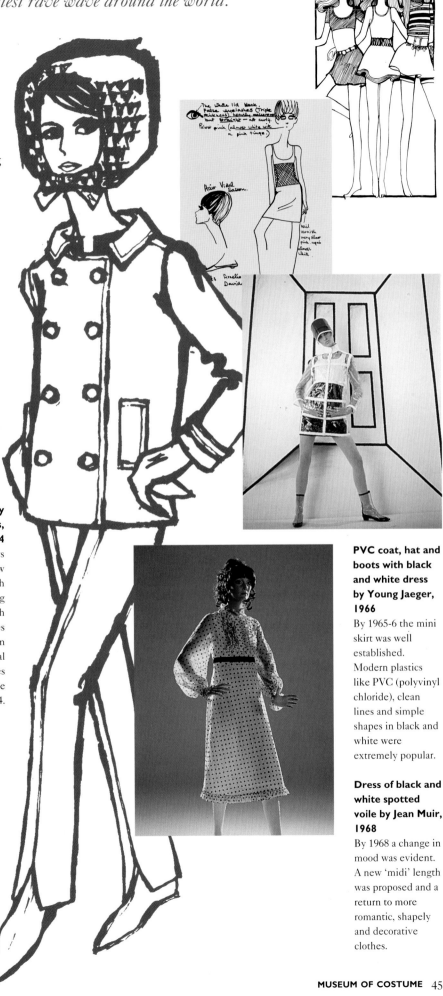

Sixties Style

The 1960s was a decade of great change. Greater freedom, opportunity and affluence for young people came with the abolition of national service, grants for higher education and full employment. Clothes began to be designed by and for the young. London in particular emerged as a new centre of original and exciting fashion. Mary Quant is the best known of this young generation of designers. Carnaby Street became famous for its fashionable boutiques.

Pop groups had an influence on men's clothes. The Beatles popularised a collarless jacket by the French designer Pierre Cardin.

Trouser suit by André Courrèges, 1964

Women's trousers were now acceptable for both day and evening wear. The French designer Courrèges launched an influential collection of clothes for the new 'Space Age' in 1964.

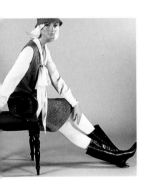

Grey tweed shift dress and chiffon blouse by Mary Quant, 1963

Chosen as the Dress of the Year for 1963, this marks a new direction for women's clothes. The waistline is no longer accentuated and the line is uncluttered. Skirts are still knee length but begin to rise in 1963.

PVC coat, hat and boots with black and white dress by Young Jaeger, 1966

By 1965-6 the mini skirt was well established. Modern plastics like PVC (polyvinyl chloride), clean lines and simple shapes in black and white were extremely popular.

Dress of black and white spotted voile by Jean Muir, 1968

By 1968 a change in mood was evident. A new 'midi' length was proposed and a return to more romantic, shapely and decorative clothes.

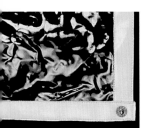

Street-style and Designer Labels

In recent decades fashion has been strongly influenced by young and alternative social groups. The Teddy Boys, Mods and Rockers of the 1950s and 1960s were followed by Hippies, Skinheads and, in the later 1970s, the Punks. Though they seemed bizarre and shocking, many 'street fashion' ideas were original and dynamic. Mainstream fashion has responded by absorbing and modifying some of these elements.

At the same time, in the prosperous and socially mobile 1980s, expensive clothes were a mark of status. The designer label became all important. For affluent young working men and women, for example, an Armani suit could signal success. This became known as 'power dressing'.

Denim

If one word could sum up fashion since the 1950s it would be denim. The phenomenon of jeans as a universal, unisex, classless, stylish, practical and inexpensive fashion dominates later-twentieth century dress. Yet denim is a traditional fabric, woven from an indigo-dyed natural fibre (cotton). Jeans began life as workmen's overalls in mid-nineteenth century America.

Denim has proved perfect for everyday wear but has also been adapted for the highest fashion garments.

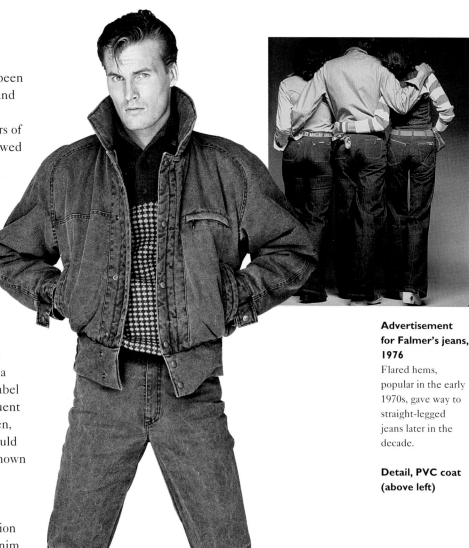

Advertisement for Falmer's jeans, 1976
Flared hems, popular in the early 1970s, gave way to straight-legged jeans later in the decade.

Detail, PVC coat (above left)

'This is the year when menswear crawled out of its fusty closet and began to dance in the streets.'
Brenda Polan, 1984

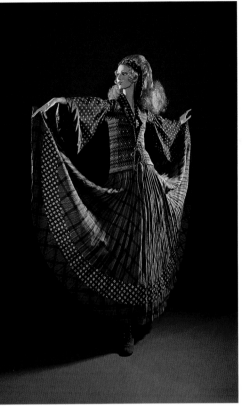

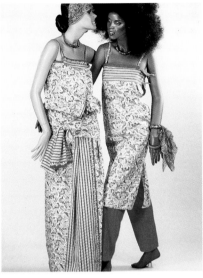

The Dress of the Year

The Museum of Costume keeps its modern collection up to date through a unique scheme. Each year since 1963 it has asked a leading fashion expert to choose a dress or outfit to represent the newest and most influential ideas in contemporary fashion. The selection is donated to the museum by the designer or maker. The result is an outstanding year by year record of recent clothes. Many of them are British but they also include the work of French, Italian, Japanese and American designers.

Blouse and skirt by Bill Gibb, waistcoat by Kaffe Fassett for Baccarat. Chosen as Dress of the Year 1970
The long skirt, full sleeves and patterned knitting reflect the romantic and ethnic tastes of the late 1960s and early 1970s.

Printed cotton summer ensembles by Kenzo Takada for Jap. Dress of the Year 1976
Kenzo's sundress and tunic and trousers illustrate the ethnic eclecticism of the time, and anticipate the fashion for separates in the latter part of the 1970s

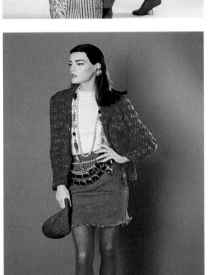

'I see denim everywhere. It is the typical look of today. It is worn with a tough leather jacket or dressed up with jewellery. Why not? It is what fashion is about, and the way fashion must go.'

Karl Lagerfeld, 1991

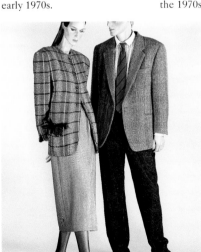

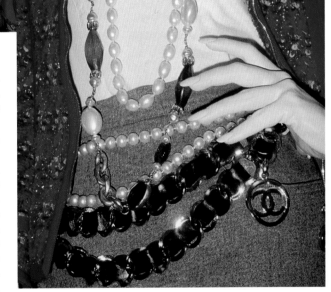

Man's and woman's clothes by Giorgio Armani. Dress of the Year, 1986
This Italian designer's clothes are noted for their stylish cut and understated elegance.

Pink lurex tweed jacket and stretch denim skirt by Karl Lagerfeld for Chanel. Dress of the Year 1991
Elements of street fashion (ripped denim, T-shirt and baseball cap) are combined with classic haute couture: Chanel's original edge to edge jacket, ropes of pearls and chain belt.

Front cover:
**Tea Room
colonnade,
Assembly Rooms**

Opposite:
**Dress of the Year
1993 by Donna
Karan**

Back cover:
**Sack-back gown of
brocaded silk, c.1770**

*This guide is published by the Heritage Services
section of Bath & North East Somerset Council
in association with the National Trust.*

*Written by Oliver Garnett and Penelope Byrde
Text pages 2–17 © 1994 The National Trust
Test pages 18–48 © 1994 Bath & North East
Somerset Council
Edited by Penelope Byrde
Designed by Bridget Heal*

*Printed in England by Barwell Colour Print Ltd
ISBN 0 901303 31 3*

*Photography by: Mandy Reynolds, Fotek, Nick Smith
and Andreas von Einsiedel (Assembly Rooms
© National Trust Photographic Library)*

*Other photographs by kind permission of:
Bath Central Library (pages 6, 7, 9, 13, 14, 15 and 16)
British Museum, London (pages 7 and 23)
Dulwich College Picture Gallery (page 13)
National Portrait Gallery, London (page 21)
Scottish National Portrait Gallery, Edinburgh (page 35)
Sir John Soane's Museum (page 4)
Victoria Art Gallery, Bath (pages 1, 2, 3, 5, 6, 8, 10, 12,
13, 14, 25 and 32)*

Drawing by Elisabeth Errington (page 28) based on
Hoops in Worthing Museum, *Daphne Bullard (1965)*
and Costume in Detail, *Nancy Bradfield (1968)*

*The assistance of the following is gratefully acknowledged:
Museum of Costume: Rosemary Harden, Rhian Tritton
and Gillian Huggins
Victoria Art Gallery: Susan Sloman
Heritage Services: Stephen Bird*

'Today's fashion – tomorrow's history.'

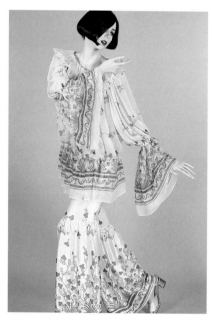

Ossie Clark, 1969

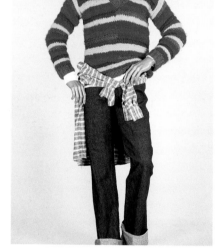

Fiorucci, 1976

Body Map, 1984

**John Galliano,
1987**

**Jean Paul Gaultier
1988**

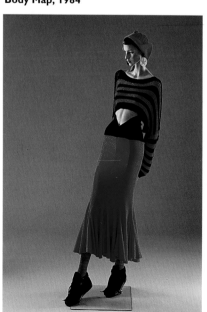

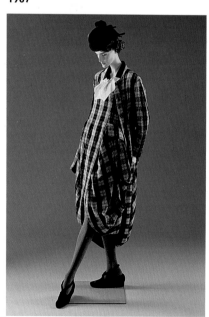

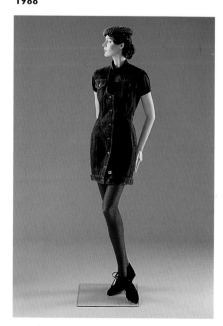